J. Yeck
L
14.10.04

Genre

Stephen Neale

1980

British Film Institute—Film Availability Services
Series Editor: Paul Willemen

Acknowledgments

I would like to thank Dinah Marmery and Ed Buscombe and Angela Martin of the BFI Educational Advisory Service for their encouragement, and Paul Willemen of the BFI Film Availability Services for his consistent support.

Cover stills: *Creature from the Black Lagoon* and *The Band Wagon.*
(Courtesy of Universal and MGM)

Contents

Presentation

by Paul Willemen

In the late sixties and early seventies, genre theory occupied a special and specific place in film theory. Its immediate context was the emergence and elaboration of a theory of cinema designed to fulfil two complementary functions.

First, it was to challenge and displace the dominant notions of cinema installed· and defended on the basis of the assumed· excellence of the 'taste' of a few journalists and reviewers, appealing to the 'age-old canons and principles' of Art in general. The notion that the 'taste' of a few educated amateurs with refined sensibilities constitutes the touchstone of film appreciation is in fact the tip of the iceberg of a complex set of propositions founded on many different institutional practices and determined by equally diverse ideological and economic factors. The most useful account of the emergence and consolidation of this impressionist dogmatism has been provided by Victor Perkins in the first chapter of his book *Film As Film* (1972) where he analysed the contradictions and components of what he called the 'established or orthodox theory of film'. Perkins commented: 'The dogma not only fails to provide a coherent basis for discussion of particular films but actively obstructs understanding of the cinema' (p. 11). As Perkins demonstrated, the dogmatically held prejudices formulated under the guise of an aesthetics of taste and personal response rested on considerations of social status: the status and prestige of cinema as an Art and therefore, by implication, the status and prestige of the film journalist-critic. Consequently, the struggle against the aesthetics of taste was simultaneously directed against the commanding heights of British film culture: the journalists signing film columns in national papers and issuing a small handful of specialised magazines. As a component of the many oppositional and democratic discourses that emerged in the late fifties and sixties, film theory began to elaborate formulations that would challenge the 'authority' and the stifling impact of the film culture establishment. The idea of a 'unique' individual responding to a 'unique' work of art was shown to be nonsensical: the critic's discourse was seen as part of a 'class' discourse while films, and especially 'popular' films, were placed in their proper context and were said to derive their strength from the contact with 'popular' traditions of art production.

Secondly, in the wake of the realisation that any form of artistic production is a rule-bound activity firmly embedded in social history, the theory of cinema set about discovering the structures which underpinned groups of films and gave them their social grounding. This is the point where the structuralist methodology, which had achieved a high degree of visibility in the French intellectual milieu in the early and mid-sixties, came in as a useful theoretical framework.

Initially, this double function of theoretical work produced an attention to the question of the author's relation to the finished product, in that 'auteurism' provided a set of problems where the requirements of the double function could

1

be condensed into a single 'problematic'. Where the orthodoxy denied the possibility of there being 'individual expression' within a film factory such as Hollywood (except for a few 'great men' who confirmed the rule by their inability to adapt: Stroheim, Chaplin, Welles), oppositional theoretical discourses gravitated towards auteurism in order to demonstrate the existence of 'individual artists' within the traditions of 'mass cinema'; at the same time, the proposition that there were authors in Hollywood required oppositional critics to have recourse to a methodology capable of demonstrating the interrelation between regularities, systemic structures at work in 'popular' cinema and specific individual, authorial signatures. The various versions of 'auteurism' that resulted, although sharing an oppositional stance *vis-à-vis* the critical establishment which enabled the formation of alliances, were deeply marked by the institutions and discourses within which they emerged and with which they entertained specific historical links. The main division within auteurism, its fault line, ran between a broadly structuralist auteurism drawing on linguistics and anthropology as well as Marx (occasionally) and an auteurism modelled on a literary ideology which, a few decades earlier, had played an equally oppositional role: Leavisism. In that triangular formation, with two different although at times overlapping forms of auteurism opposing the subjectivist dogmas of the establishment, genre theory was produced in a 'critical', in all senses of the term, place within film theory. 'Genre', often appearing cloaked under the pejorative term 'formula', was the magic word used by the establishment to found their allegation that 'popular' cinema was a mass-produced factory product devoid of 'personality'. 'Genre' films could be enjoyed as 'entertainment' whenever the refined critic felt like slumming or aggressively affirming his or her status as just an 'ordinary' person entitled to speak in the name of 'the people'. The literary auteurists didn't question the notion that art was a matter of individual talent, but argued that the marks of such talent were evident even within the most rigorously codified genres such as westerns or gangster films. In that sense, genre-structure and author-structure were seen as concepts of a different order existing side by side, with genre providing a framework, a 'tradition' within which and against which individuality could flourish. The linguistics-based auteurists mobilised the great tradition of Russian and Czech formalism and, although not explicitly antagonistic to notions of individual specificity, at least succeeded in beginning to displace the focus of attention away from individualism towards theoretical issues regarding the structure of artistic texts in general. It was structuralist auteurism that put the notion of meaning production on the agenda and programmed the appeal to semiology as the discipline that was to account for the way texts work as signifying structures.

However, together with this displacement away from problems of the 'artist' towards problems of text construction and the issues raised in that context, the concept of genre also lost its critical function in that it became marginalised, no longer located at the 'critical' nexus of the arguments between auteurists and establishment. No longer was it a matter of individual versus formula/genre, or of author-within-genre-framework, but of disengaging the various different levels and codes, the various systems of signification at work within any given

2

text or group of texts. The distinctions between such groups were no longer formulated in terms of genres, but in terms of narrative/non-narrative; illusionist/anti-illusionist; classic/modernist, etc. This shift, a logical working through of some of the problems inherent in auteurism, in turn required the other discourses (subjectivists and literary auteurists) to reformulate their own positions in relation to the new critical conjuncture.

Of course, these few notes provide an overly schematic and somewhat reductive account of the complexity of the discourses at play over the past two decades, and there are many instances of mixed discourses that partake to varying degrees of all three main discursive/ideological practices. However, such a schematic account at least allows for a clearer understanding of why auteurism proved the least difficult element to accommodate within establishment criticism which, by means of this recovery manoeuvre, re-established its massive dominance, relegating the Leavisite variant to the realms of formal educational institutions and the semiological-psychoanalytic developments of film theory to the fringes of radical academicism. By absorbing some elements of auteurism, the journalistic establishment in effect made genre theory redundant and regained its position at relatively little cost. Only the stress on theoretical rigour and the attention to the workings of signifying systems called for by the linguistic-auteurists remained radically impossible to accommodate within dominant reviewing practices.

The immediate impact on genre theory was that, as a result of the shift in the relations of force in the critical conjuncture, it got caught up in the tendency towards the formulation of a structuralist-inspired theory of cinema, thus losing its polemical charge. However, a further shift programmed its virtual disappearance from the critical agenda. Under the women's movement's impact on questions of cultural/ideological struggle and the movement's direct political engagement with questions of representation, formal structuralism (semiology or film semiotics) was seen to be inadequate because unable to address the issues raised in the context of feminism: the construction of the sexed subject in history through discursive practices (amongst others). This time, the shift was even further away from the kind of concerns and issues that had presided over the emergence of genre theory. In the mid-seventies, while establishment dogma was incorporating some aspects of the cruder forms of auteurism, oppositional theoretical work concentrated on the need to account for cinema as a specific signifying practice involving questions regarding the relation between texts and viewers (problem of the look, questions of address and subject construction, problem of identification/distanciation, etc.). This relation set the terms for considerations which have preoccupied film theory for the last four years or so. However, the dangers inherent in this development were many: a complete loss of contact with 'dominant' film culture, combined with requirements to make a living in academic contexts under adverse circumstances (economic and ideological attacks on all forms of 'progressive' education), has resulted in a tendency towards theoreticism and forms of radical opportunism. Examples of this development can be seen in the emergence of notions such as the proposition that 'subjects' are hopelessly and helplessly adrift on a sea of discursiveness, the 'forgetting' or even the rejection of economic determinants on discursive practices; the dissolution of the 'individual text' as a valid object of study (a development that, although theoretically justifiable, guaranteed the loss of contact with dominant forms of film culture that need to be displaced), the belief that discourse in and by itself constitutes an 'autonomous' practice (junking the problem symptomatically indicated in the Althusserian formulation of 'relative autonomy' of the ideological *vis-à-vis* the political and the economic) determined by the logic of the signifier, or, alternatively, the systematic and self-referential circulation of concepts, thus making discursive activities immune from the necessity of planning and strategy in favour of a radical a-historicist opportunism that abdicated, in theory, any responsibility for the effects discursive practices may have.

As these tendencies became more pronounced within theoretical work, the need to find a terrain on which dominant discourses could be challenged more directly became more urgent. This took the form of, on the one hand, attempts to link oppositional theoretical work with forms of oppositional cinema (the work of the Edinburgh Film Festival since 1975 stands out in this respect) and on the other, a return to an engagement with problems of narrative and, eventually, genre as an issue within this work on narrative. However, it may be misleading to speak of a 'return', as the current work on genre in no way ignores or deprecates the theoretical work that has been achieved over the last five years or so. It is a return through the prism of that work, an attempt to rethink problems in terms of the theory of discourse that emerged in the meantime. Moreover, the overall thrust of this work, still in its initial stages, is characterised by its attempt to reconnect with the various issues that circulate in educational institutions and that inform various aspects of contemporary film making, both in its mainstream and in its oppositional variants.

Within the last two years, a number of critics/theorists have begun to formulate this need to rethink genre theory: Antony Easthope and Mike Westlake in Manchester (some of their work will be published shortly in *North by Northwest*, no 8 and in *Screen Education*, nos 32/33), while in London, working in parallel, Steve Neale attempted to renegotiate the whole issue from within a theoretical problematic which turns on the consideration of signification in terms of modes of address and discursive strategies. Steve Neale's work, as presented in this booklet, provides an initial clearing of the ground and a setting out of some crucial parameters. It is not offered as a comprehensive new theory of genre, merely as a sketch of what such a theory might look like and what problems it should be able to account for. In that respect, this booklet is very much part of a work in progress, part of a first phase of what hopefully will become a renewed attention to the problem of cinematic genre. As such, this booklet is conceived as a focus for educational and exhibition practices such as the organisation of seasons and seminars, preferably in conjunction with each other, suggesting lines for further work, areas that need further elaboration or perhaps even fundamental reformulation.

4

Introduction

Theoretical work on the concept of genre in the cinema and theoretically informed work on individual genres began to be developed in Britain mainly in the late sixties and early seventies, a period which saw the publication of, in particular, an issue of *Screen* (Vol 11, no 2) containing the two articles *The Notion of Genre* by Tom Ryall and *The Idea of Genre in the American Cinema* by Ed Buscombe, and of the books *Horizons West* by Jim Kitses and *Underworld USA* by Colin McArthur. The impulses behind this work were largely twofold: on the one hand a desire to maintain and extend critical interest in mainstream, commercial—particularly Hollywood—cinema; on the other hand, a desire to qualify what had been up to that time the dominant critical method for discussing that area of cinema seriously, namely auteurism In fact, this work on genre remained and continues to remain undeveloped. Very little has been published since that has sought to extend it, either through a more systematic working out and application of the concepts and ideas it had already developed, or through a coherent critique and subsequent transformation of these concepts and ideas.

Only two recently published articles can be said genuinely to discuss genre from within the conceptual framework originally mapped out by this work, *Genre and Movies* by Douglas Pye in *Movie* no 20, and *Teaching Through Genre* by Tom Ryall in *Screen Education* no 17, Winter 1975/76. There are a number of reasons for this apparent lack of productivity. The work I am referring to coincided with the introduction of structuralism and semiotics into Britain, and, indeed, to some extent referred to and drew upon its concepts. Increasingly, structuralism and semiotics focused either on the single, individual text, or on the general principles of signification and the politics of signifying practices, thereby effectively excluding the priority of the specification and analysis of genre and genres. Moreover, structuralism and semiotics together with Althusserian and post-Althusserian Marxism, which contributed fundamentally to the transformation of the analysis of the cinema through its insistence on the importance of theory, its critique of empiricism and sociology, its insistence on the importance of ideology within the sphere of the social formation and through the general political impetus it gave to film culture, served to problematise the conceptual field within which the work of the genre critics was located.

What this booklet aims to do is to relocate the discussion of and the importance accorded to genre, hence to rework, re-place and to a large extent transform the basic terms and concepts used in and promoted by that discussion. On the one hand, this will involve a critique of the work of the genre critics, and on the other a set of reformulations in the light of the overlapping but by no means homogeneously co-existent fields of semiotics, psychoanalysis and post-Althusserian Marxism, each of which finds its focus in a set of problems generally designated by the term ideology. More specifically, this set of reformulations and transformations bears on the notion of cinema as a set of social practices, that is to say, it centres round the issues and problems involved in the analysis of the cinema as a social institution. Attending to these problems also implies consideration, firstly, of the filmic text as a signifying process involving specific aesthetic systems and subjective processes, and, secondly, of the differential social determinants and effects involved in distinct forms and practices of cinema. To that extent, this booklet is intended for a readership interested in these problems and hence in the politics of the film culture in which they are embedded and from which they find their impetus.

Finally, it should be said that the particular sequencing of the discussion of genre adopted in this booklet as a whole is governed by principles of exposition rather than by any hierarchy of importance accorded to the various issues discussed. Moreover, given the space and framework of a booklet rather than a full-length book, and given the exploratory nature of much of that discussion, the treatment of these issues will be varied and uneven. Again, this should not be taken as an indication of their relative importance or theoretical weight.

Chapter 1

In a succinct and useful article on genre, focusing on the discussion of a particular genre film, *The Searchers*, and on the ways in which genre can be taught, Tom Ryall reviews previous work on the subject in the light of the following basic orientation:

> 'The master image for genre criticism is the triangle composed of artist/film/audience. Genres may be defined as patterns/forms/styles/structures which transcend individual films, and which supervise both their construction by the film maker, and their reading by an audience.'[1]

The problem here is that while an interrelationship central to an understanding of genre is clearly located, i.e. the triangle 'artist/film/audience', there are no conceptual means offered for its analysis. There is no sense in which Ryall proposes a conception of audience and film maker as either self-consistent, autonomous instances of subjectivity or as simple empirical entities in their respective relations to the 'patterns/forms/styles/structures' of genre. However, the term he uses to indicate the mechanism(s) involved in these relations— 'supervise'—while suggesting its supra-personal force, fails to provide the conceptual apparatus necessary for its further specification.

This is a common and fundamental problem with the genre criticism under consideration here. Given a lack of the theoretical means for thinking the force of aesthetic systems such as genre in relation to the instances of subjectivity referred to via the terms 'film maker' and 'audience', the way is open for the ideology of a transcendent, self-consistent subject implicit in the simple communication model of author-text/system-audience which tends to propose itself as a means of filling a conceptual gap. This is overtly evident in, for instance, Jim Kitses' definition of an aesthetic convention as 'an area of agreement between audience and artist'[2] and in the following remarks by Colin McArthur on the potential importance of genre for a semiotics of the cinema:

> '. . . genre, with its obvious analogy with a sign-system, *an agreed code* between film maker and audience, would seem on the face of it a fruitful starting point for investigating the semiology of the cinema.'[3]

This ideology only surfaces at certain points in these texts. Indeed, it is often in contradiction with statements which imply that generic conventions have a force of their own, independent of the conscious will of either film maker or audience. McArthur, for instance, in another passage in *Underworld USA*, writes as follows:

> 'There has been a curious reluctance among film critics to confront the notion of genre, the most usual reason offered being that genres are collections of neutral conventions which the director either animates or not, according to his qualities as a director. If he is Nicholas Ray, he transcends the genre; if he is Edward Dmytryk, he makes just another western. This

7

position seems at odds with the importance placed on genre by both film makers and audiences. The responses of film makers and audiences to the genres seem to offer a good prima facie case for believing that they are animating rather than neutral, that they carry an intrinsic charge of meaning independently of whatever is brought to them by particular directors.' (p. 19)

The contradiction is even evident within the space of a few sentences in *Horizons West:*

> 'The western is not just the men who have worked within it. Rather than an empty vessel breathed into by the film maker, the genre is a vital structure through which flow a myriad of themes and concepts. As such the form can provide a director with a range of possible connections and the space in which to experiment, to shape and refine the kind of effects and meanings he is working towards.' (p. 26)

Here reference is made to what McArthur calls the 'intrinsic charge' borne by generic conventions, yet that charge is circumscribed as external to the subjectivity of the director, who thus remains an autonomous identity, able simply to 'experiment, to shape and refine' within the framework that generic conventions provide.

Reinforcing this contradiction, blocking any resolution that may potentially exist through a rethinking of the ideology of subjectivity involved in the conceptualisation of the relation between subject and convention, is a distinction between high art and popular art whose premises include a demarcation between the conditions of creativity involved in each case, the degree of 'contact' between artist and audience, and the degree of autonomy and/or control *vis-à-vis* the art work and its constituent materials. As such, the distinction in fact rests on a fundamentally complicit acceptance of the basis of 'high art' ideologies: i.e. that the artist has a self-consistent, potentially autonomous and transcendent self and that art is its (more or less realised) expression. The only argument concerns the value to be placed on pure self-expression (high art) on the one hand, and self-expression mediated by established conventions (popular art) on the other:

> 'The conventions of . . . genre are known and recognised by the audience, and such recognition is in itself a pleasure. Popular art, in fact, has always depended on this: one might argue that the modern idea of novelty (or 'originality') as a major, even *the* major, quality to be desired in a work of art dates from the Romantic period. And as Raymond Williams shows in *Culture and Society*, it is during this period that art began to move away from its contact with a large, roughly homogeneous audience. We have there the beginnings of the present-day division between 'mass' and 'highbrow' culture. All too easily this originality degenerates into eccentricity and communication is sacrificed in the interests of self-expression. It is one of the chief merits of the American cinema that this has, on the whole, not yet happened.'[4]

'Self-expression' exists as a possibility; it is just that it is not fully to be valued for its own sake. The contradiction of this position—the way in which it seeks to distance itself from the ideology of high art, yet the way in which it remains fundamentally complicit with it at the level of the conceptualisation of the artistic subject—is especially evident in those instances where work on genre is articulated polemically as a counterweight to auteurism. The basis of that polemic is not a hostility to the ideology of the subject implicit in auteurism— at least not in its traditional forms—it is rather that auteurism is viewed as inappropriate in the context of the commercial cinema, since the working conditions obtaining there preclude the kinds of control and autonomy thought to be available to, and characteristic of, the artist working in the field of high culture. The latter is free of the constraints of commerce and of the conventional and formulaic nature of commercially-oriented aesthetic forms; the former has to contend with these constraints and they inevitably qualify and modify the full, untrammelled expression of the self:

'. . . rejection of Hollywood and its values, though understandable and even laudable, has led to a rejection of American movies which is neither. When one discusses literature or painting and, up to a point, drama, one can place the artist, his work and his audience in a very direct relationship. However, no such direct relationship with his work and his audience exists for the director in Hollywood. There are at work several *modifiers of meaning*, factors which complicate these relationships. The most obvious are the star system and the subject of this book, genre—both, of course, partly explicable in terms of the overpoweringly commercial basis of Hollywood production.'[5]

Not only does this kind of position ultimately work to confirm the ideology of subjectivity fundamental to high art, but, by mapping a high art/popular art distinction across a distinction between 'commercial' and 'non-commercial' it effectively precludes a recognition, and hence a potential analysis, of the (different) ways in which all forms of artistic production in capitalist social formations take place within conditions provided by capitalist economic relations and practices and hence the ways in which the production and consumption of all art works are conditioned by commodity forms.

Tom Ryall's article, too, is finally blocked by its own premises and by the contradictions they involve:

'One of the major impulses behind genre criticism lies in the common sense assumption that commercial films are produced according to generic formulae, that film tradition and the history of the cinema play an important role in determining the actual specificity of any single American picture. The 'auteur theory', though important and valuable during the 1950s and 1960s for drawing attention to the importance of the American cinema, nevertheless tended to treat popular art *as if* it were 'high culture'. *Thus* Hollywood films were discussed in terms of their director's personal vision, world view, individual style and so on.'[6] (My emphases)

The discussion of 'personal vision, world view, individual style' is appropriate and acceptable within the field of high culture but not within the field of popular culture simply because the production conditions pertaining in the latter are marked by certain constraints. Among those constraints are the conventions of genre and certain forms of dramatic narrative, which act to mediate between the artist's self and the audience he/she addresses. Such constraints exist only because of the specific economic conditions of production, distribution and exhibition within the commercial cinema and of the size and heterogeneity of the audience involved, and hence because of the pressure on the one hand to facilitate 'communication' and on the other hand to maximise the profitability of capital assets and to repeat the formulae marking previous financial successes. The corollary of this is that other forms of artistic production, distribution and consumption do not involve, at the level of signification and the production of meaning, the kinds of supra-personal pressure inherent in the conventions of genre which Ryall attempts to encapsulate in his notion of 'supervision'. All forms of signification and meaning entail pressure: no subject is transcendent of such pressure or in control of its various modalities, hence no subject is in a position simply to operate these forms, whatever the conditions of production and consumption, whatever the form of economic relations within which production and consumption take place. Indeed, such pressure is precisely one of the most important of those conditions. Its modalities may vary within different signifying media and within different aesthetic systems, processes and ideologies across these media. But, as regards the fundamental fact of this pressure, no artist—and, indeed, no audience, no individual spectator or reader—is free, and this applies equally to the abstract expressionist painter, to the lyric poet working in his/her own home or studio, to the experimental film maker working only in 8mm and to the Hollywood director. It is at this point, given this overall framework of premises, and precisely, in a sense, because of it, that it becomes important, indeed essential, to differentiate between the various modalities of pressure involved, and to relate them to the various modalities of the political, ideological and economic conditions in which they function and take effect. Generic conventions and the genre form itself should be viewed as one of the variants of the modalities of that pressure.

If the pressure of genre conventions is to some extent recognised but not adequately conceptualised and specified, it is similarly the case that while the existence of those conventions is central to genre criticism and theory, they too are rarely specified and analysed in detail and in ways which recognise their specific autonomy and their role in the constitution of genre as an aesthetic category. Ryall, for instance, refers rather loosely to genres as 'patterns/forms/styles/structures which transcend individual films', and the bulk of the work to which he refers has generally restricted itself to the discussion of the particular and limited area of the aesthetics of genre usually termed 'iconography'. Iconography has received particular attention because it was felt to be concerned specifically with the role of 'the visual' in genre films, and that an analysis of iconography would therefore make possible an engagement with a number of the specificities of film.

The problem with the concept of iconography—and with the uses to which it has been put—is not that it does not fully correspond to the concept specified by the term in the field of art history from which it derives. It is rather that it is loosely and imprecisely defined within the field of cinema. Ed Buscombe, for instance, uses the term simply as a synonym for 'visual conventions', themselves unspecified in general terms, and Colin McArthur similarly refers to iconography simply as 'patterns of visual imagery'. Because of this imprecision the analytical categories it is capable of generating are insufficient to differentiate between a number of distinct levels within the field of 'the visual', and within either an individual genre film or a genre as a whole, and hence of specifying the distinct and different functions which the elements it *is* capable of isolating serve to perform within them. McArthur, for example, divides the 'patterns of imagery' characteristic of the gangster film/thriller into the following categories:

> 'those surrounding the physical presence, attributes and dress of the actors and the characters they play; those emanating from the milieux within which the characters operate; and those connected with the technology at the characters' disposal.'[7]

To begin with, it is worth asking to what degree these categories can be used in the analysis of genres other than the gangster film/thriller. To what degree, therefore, are they capable of integration within a general theory of genre as a whole? How would the third category, for instance, apply to the musical or the melodrama—what is the force of the term 'technology' within this category? A second point to note is the central role of 'character' in the construction of these categories: it serves *a priori* to exclude consideration of the structures and processes of narrative, whether these be specific to the genre in question or not, and to their role in the generation of the meanings signified by the elements to which he draws attention. Thirdly, as I have already suggested, it allows elements to be either differentiated in accordance with the criteria governing the construction of the different categories, or to be grouped together within them in a way which is both too rigid and too arbitrary. The same elements are capable of performing a number of distinct textual functions and can be grouped within a number of different categories. Thus, within the gangster/thriller genre, machine guns and pistols could be characterised under the heading 'technology at the characters' disposal'. Equally, however, they may function so as to contribute to a definition of the attributes of a character. For instance in *Baby Face Nelson*, Mickey Rooney's machine gun is an essential component in the signification of his attributes as a character at a number of levels, and in the case of the various roles played by James Cagney, that actor's attributes of 'physical dynamism' and 'ruthlessness' as defined by McArthur are at least partly signified by the weaponry he employs and the actions he performs with it. On the other hand, as McArthur himself states, 'firearms, automobiles and telephones', which must surely be included under the category of 'technology at the characters' disposal', are part of the 'complex technology of the city'. As such they are equally part of the iconography of the city 'milieu' whose imagery is otherwise said to constitute a separate iconographical category.

What I am arguing is not that each of the functions performed by particular elements should be exhaustively specified, but that, firstly, there should be a recognition that elements are capable of performing a number of different and distinct functions, and, secondly, that any categorisation of these elements should proceed in accordance with criteria that are explicitly formulated in relation to a specific function and that the theoretical reasons for the privilege accorded to that function be spelt out. This is not the case in the example from *Underworld USA* discussed above, nor indeed in the bulk of the discussion of generic iconography in cinema. Furthermore, none of the elements grouped together by McArthur are simply and strictly 'visual', whatever the merits or demerits of the way in which they are classified; firstly, because the narrative structures in which they find their place are precisely structures rather than aggregates of empirically visible phenomena, and, secondly, because in any case the matters of expression across which the signifiers of character, milieu, technology, etc. are distributed include not only the moving photographic image, but also recorded musical sound, recorded phonetic sound, recorded noises and graphic material such as writing (titles, intertitles and so on). Thus it both fails in its aim of engaging the specificity of film while simultaneously foreclosing the specification and analysis of generic conventions which are not particular to the cinema and their interaction and interrelation with those that are. This is due primarily to the criteria adopted to motivate the concept of iconography and to the basis for those criteria, outlined and given a polemical edge by Buscombe in the following terms:

> 'Since we are dealing with a visual medium we ought surely to look for our defining criteria at what we actually see on the screen.'[8]

This basis is both too broad, disallowing sufficient logical differentiation within the field it delimits, and too narrow, disallowing discussion and differentiation of what is extraneous to that field. Furthermore, it introduces a demarcation and division between the field of iconography and the field of theme and signified meaning. This division both reproduces the form/content dichotomy and motivates that dichotomy on empirical and largely arbitrary grounds. Hence what could be argued to be important or even central conventions of a number of genres are discussed under the heading of 'theme' or 'ideology' rather than as conventional structures. So, when McArthur refers to the rise and fall structure of *Little Caesar*, *Public Enemy* and *Scarface*, conceptualising the fact that the gangster figure must ultimately die in each of the films not only in terms of thematics but also in terms of narrative convention, and when Kitses talks of narrative motifs and situations in *Horizons West*, it is in each case in contradiction to the general conceptual framework that they initially erected. As a result, the points made and examples given are not susceptible to sustained and systematic theoretical analysis.

In an unpublished paper on iconography, its derivation from and meaning within the field of art history and its subsequent deployment within genre theory and criticism,[9] Colin McArthur provides a useful and pertinent critique of the limitations, imprecisions and confusions surrounding the term. He points out both the way in which its usage has been tied to the form/content dichotomy and the way in which it can serve to block analysis of cinematic specificity. The following passage from the paper is worth quoting at some length:

'It seems clear that the art historical notion of iconography has been applied to the cinema somewhat crudely, without due regard for the problems raised by the specificity of the cinema. For example, a simple two tier notion of art as form and content underlies most iconographical writing in art history, with the iconographer leaning in the direction of content. But surely the cinema requires a more sophisticated model than that of form/content. The necessary sophistication has been added by Paul Willemen in his notion of the pro-filmic event (itself a collection of sign-events) which is staged for no other reason than to be acted upon by the codes of the cinema (all the functions of the camera, lighting, cutting, sound, colour) in the process of film making.

With a model such as that offered by Willemen, the area of applicability for the notion of iconography in the movies becomes clearer: that is, it becomes subsumed into the process of decoding the various sign-events of the pro-filmic event. . . . (Thus) the term might still be useful to describe programmed recurrences at this level, e.g. in gesture, attributes, dress, milieu, objects and events. As such, iconography would have a claim to attention no greater or less than that of programmed recurrences at the formal level of the cinema (e.g. the closeup, the flashback, etc.).'

Thus McArthur both specifies the place of iconography within the field of 'the visual' and delimits the degree of its importance. However, the recurrence of the term 'formal' ('the formal level of the cinema') is symptomatic of the recurrence of the fundamental problem of the form-content dichotomy, even though there is an explicit attempt to criticise and establish a conceptual distance from it.

The problem with the form/content opposition is that it remains a dichotomy rather than becoming a dialectical relation. It both produces and is produced by a conception of both texts and textual systems as products rather than as processes of production, a conception which can thus only deal with structure at the expense of structuration, with enounced at the expense of enunciation, with static, that is to say, listable entities rather than with elements whose constitution as relatively 'stable' generic components is a result of their function in a constant process of repetition and difference. In such a process, repetition is never simply the return of the identical and difference is never simply the eruption of the absolutely new. What is needed here is theoretical specification of these mechanisms, both at the level of the individual generic text and at the level of supra-textual, generic systems. It is from here that the nature and function of 'generic conventions' can be specified and that the nature, place and function of 'generic iconography' can be located.

Reference has already been made to the role of Hollywood as commercial/industrial institution in the constitution of a number of aspects of genre: the way in which Hollywood's structures and practices entail both a formulaic aesthetic and, as a corollary, a whole set of constraints/disciplines upon the film makers working there. This role and the precise nature of these structures and practices is rarely examined in great detail. Tom Ryall's article in *Screen Education* perhaps contains the lengthiest and fullest exposition:

'Films are, and have been from the earliest days of Hollywood, produced and marketed as westerns, comedies and so on; in addition, such categories are part and parcel of the film reviewer's vocabulary, and the popular audience uses such divisions to guide its film viewing. That the commercial cinema organises its production along generic lines is, therefore, confirmed at the level of common sense through our everyday experience of the cinema but it may also be confirmed by examining the commercial structure of Hollywood. The standardisation of product obliged by the economic necessities of large scale industrial production led to particular studios concentrating on particular genres, and indeed, building up teams of stars, directors, writers and so on, for that purpose.'[10]

This quotation is particularly interesting, both for negative and for positive reasons. In common with the body of genre theory and criticism to which it refers and upon which it draws, it fails to link a number of the features of the economic structures and practices involved to capitalist economic practices and structures in general. In this way, it operates to block, firstly, any further analysis of them, secondly, any attempt to locate them within the social formation as a whole or, thirdly, to locate them within those economic features of the social formation which are conjuncturally specific. On the other hand, it fails to conceptualise the relation(s) between such structures and practices and the specific genres and generic cycles that actually have existed. Or rather, it posits a fairly direct relationship between economic structures and practices and the existence of genre while failing to lay the foundations for analyses which would be able to link such a premise to the existence of specific genres and specific generic cycles.

One of the central issues involved here is that of the conceptualisation of discourse, of 'institution' and of the economic as an instance of the social formation. Consequently, it becomes impossible to analyse or even to think the various relations between these agencies. The potential for dealing with this issue is, to some degree, present in Ryall's article. For instance, regarding Hollywood as an institution, reference is made not only to specific economic structures and practices in the sphere of production, but also to a category of marketing which potentially includes discursive though non-cinematic elements such as advertising strategies, posters, stills, trade reviews, trade synopses, reviewing and so on. All these areas of practice are seen as contributing fundamentally to the demarcation of genres, the establishing of categories and classifications within the social process of cinema as a whole. The inclusion of these elements, overlapping with the practices of the industry *stricto sensu* but also extending beyond them, is extremely important. Its consequences are not thought through, but a recognition of the fact that a whole set of different elements are at play within the catch-all phrase of 'the social process' is an essential first step in

14

reconstituting what is meant by the 'institution' of cinema, and thus to unblock a number of the contradictions dogging the work of the genre theorists and critics.

As it is, however, the contradictions that mark Ryall's text and function as a block within it, particularly in relation to the differential treatment of genre and genres, necessitate a recourse to the concept of an origin:

'We can approach questions of the way in which the studio structure, the star system and so on may constitute the empirical roots from which a genre may grow.'[11]

The concept of an origin, the 'empirical roots', appears in order to attempt to resolve the genre-genres contradiction by introducing a point at which the economic practices viewed as defining the existence and structure of genre in general (especially those aesthetic elements which are marked by marks of repetition such as conventional formulae, iconography and so on) simultaneously give rise to the particular genres that actually have existed together with their specific aesthetic characteristics. The recourse to the concept of an origin can also be found in the attempt to resolve another problem which partly arises because of that same contradiction. The wish to resolve this contradiction not only gives rise to general statements concerning the possibility of accounting for the existence of specific genres and conventions solely on the basis of the economic practices of the industry, as in the passage from Ryall quoted above. It also gives rise to a wish to motivate their existence within the context of socio-historical 'reality'. The specific contradiction involved here hinges on a desire to investigate and to respect the discursive specificity of Hollywood films on the one hand, and yet, on the other, a desire to socially locate that specificity. This remains a contradiction because discursive specificity is not fully addressed, something upon which any broader social location of specific discourses would have to depend. Instead genre films and their conventions tend to be collapsed into the 'reality' which is held to motivate them. Hence, two impulses are constantly at odds, their mutual incidence engendering a further set of contradictions, most notably between general statements with regard to a genre and its socio-historical 'roots' and particular analyses of specific genre films and conventions. It also gives rise, to some degree at least, to the frequently noted discrepancy within *Horizons West* and *Underworld USA* between the general chapters on genre and the chapters devoted to the work of particular directors, which is precisely where films, their structures and their meanings are discussed in detail and at some length. It is the attempt to resolve these contradictions that again entails the recourse to the concept of an origin, a mythical point at which discourse and 'reality' meet, a point in 'reality', outside particular texts or discourses, at which the contradictions disappear, at which 'reality' engenders texts and discourses. This is especially evident in Ed Buscombe's article, perhaps because it is a text which seeks to engage most fully and systematically with the specificity of genre conventions in cinema. One particular section is devoted to the problem of the relation between the western and American history, arguing that the specificity of the genre be located within the 'outer form of visual conventions' rather than within the particular relation a genre like the western may have with socio-historical reality:

> 'We are not bound to make any very close connections between the western genre and historical reality. Of course there *are* connections. But too many discussions of these problems fall down over this point because it is usually assumed that the relationship must be a direct one; that since in fact there was a West, westerns must be essentially concerned with it. Kitses, for instance, states that "the basic convention of the genre is that films in western guise are about America's past". This is simply not true of many of the films, including several of the ones he discusses, for only Peckinpah of his three directors is at all preoccupied with historical themes.'[12]

None the less, the article draws to a close as follows:

> 'The question of the relation between the western and history, which I have argued is by no means simple, and not always central, *can only be answered with certainty* when we know how the form *began*.' (My emphases)

Buscombe's approach here, or rather his refusal to locate genres in accordance with their diegetic referent, differentiates his article from the other books and articles to which I have referred. It enables him to develop a general theory of genre conventions and iconography and thus to pose the possibility of analysing genres such as the horror film and the musical, which are rarely mentioned at all, primarily because of the empirical way in which genres are approached, but also because of the pervasive presence of the genre-reality issue posed in terms which constantly seek to locate determinants for aesthetic forms in non-aesthetic events.

Finally, it is worth turning to a passage from *Underworld USA* which contains an interesting ambiguity of which one component could provide the beginnings of a solution to the overall contradictions in which it is caught:

> 'The western and the gangster film have a special relationship with American society. Both deal with critical phases of American history. It could be said that they represent America talking to itself about, in the case of the western, its agrarian past, and in the case of the gangster film/thriller, its urban technological present.'[13]

There is clearly a split here between society/history as that which motivates the western and the gangster film/thriller, and a conception in which these genres function to signify meanings in the present about either the past or the present itself. In other words, there is an acknowledgment that genres and their meanings have an active role and a social effectivity of their own, to the extent that they function actively as components within the construction of socio-historical reality, rather than simply as reflections of it. They are determining factors, not simply determined ones.

However, the full exploration of this potentiality and the full theorisation of its consequences is blocked by the overall framework in which it arises: a framework marked by a problem pointed to above and which perhaps can be said to overdetermine most of the other problems and contradictions to which I have attempted to draw attention. This is the problem of the conception of signification which the various texts adopt, that is to say, a notion of signification constantly caught in the form/content dichotomy. Hence, Tom Ryall notes the contradiction in the passage from *Underworld USA* quoted above, and a similar one in *Horizons West,* but his formulation in each case is that at these points the text 'blurs the distinction between the first category of historical/social "raw material" and the second category of thematic constructions.'[14]

The point here is that this formulation, though it notes the contradiction and, indeed, points to its potential productivity, in fact precludes any further development and resolution of it by conceiving it as a contradiction between 'historical/social "raw material"' and 'thematic constructions'. A genuine development, clarification and resolution of the contradiction would have to entail not simply an attention to the specificity of generic themes but also an attention to the mechanisms of signification involved in the very constitution, not only of genre themes, but also of genres as such. And it is this which is blocked by the theme/iconography dichotomy, as it is itself a product of the lack of a theory of signification as process, regardless of the level at which the analysis is pitched: whether it focuses on the relations of film maker and audience, on specific filmic texts, on supra-textual systems, or whether the analysis attempts to grapple with aspects of the social formation as a whole.

In a sense, each of the problems I have tried to isolate and the issues they raise can be summed up in relation to, and as a function of, that with which I began this chapter: the problem of specifying the various mechanisms and the various levels of analysis involved in Ryall's notion of 'supervision'. What is required is a set of concepts with which the pressure of genre can begin to be located: in terms of the relations of subjectivity involved; in terms of the structures and practices both of the cinematic institution as a whole and of that sector known variously as 'Hollywood' or as 'the commercial cinema'; and in terms of the determinants and effects of each of these within and across the social formation and its component areas. In a booklet of this size, I cannot hope to deal exhaustively with each of these issues. But what I aim to do is to outline the conceptual field within which the components of this pressure can begin to be specified and to deal at some length with one or two of them.

Notes

[1] Tom Ryall, 'Teaching Through Genre' in *Screen Education* no 17, p. 28.
[2] J. Kitses, *Horizons West*, London 1969, p. 24.
[3] C. McArthur, *Underworld USA*, London 1972, p. 20.
[4] E. Buscombe, 'The Idea of Genre in the American Cinema' in *Screen*, Vol 11, no 2, p. 43.
[5] C. McArthur, op. cit., p. 13.
[6] T. Ryall, op. cit., p. 28.
[7] C. McArthur, op. cit., p. 24.
[8] E. Buscombe, op. cit., p. 36.
[9] C. McArthur, *Iconography and Iconology*, British Film Institute Educational Advisory Service/Society for Education in Film and Television, seminar paper, 1973.
[10] T. Ryall, op. cit., p. 27.
[11] T. Ryall, op. cit., p. 28.
[12] E. Buscombe, op. cit., pp. 39–40.
[13] C. McArthur, *Underworld USA*, p. 18.
[14] T. Ryall, op. cit., p. 30.

Chapter 2

The cinema is not simply an industry or a set of individual texts. Above all, it is a social institution. As Christian Metz writes in *The Imaginary Signifier*:

> 'The cinematic institution is not just the cinema industry (which works to fill cinemas, not to empty them), it is also the mental machinery—another industry—which spectators "accustomed to the cinema" have internalised historically and which has adapted them to the consumption of films'.[1]

Not only a set of economic practices or meaningful products, cinema is also a constantly fluctuating series of signifying processes, a 'machine' for the production of meanings and positions, or rather positionings for meaning; a machine for the regulation of the orders of subjectivity. Genres are components in this 'machine'. As systematised forms of the articulation of meaning and position, they are a fundamental part of the cinema's 'mental machinery'. Approached in this way, genres are not to be seen as forms of textual codifications, but as systems of orientations, expectations and conventions that circulate between industry, text and subject.

In this context, a number of points should be stressed. Firstly, cinema involves a plurality of operations and processes. The term 'machine' refers less to a single englobing operation across the whole field of cinema or across the whole of the social formation in which it finds its historically varying place, than to the plurality of channels, demarcated spaces and orders of regularity that underpin signifying practices. It refers to the way in which each of these practices is constantly classified, separated and differentiated in order to produce a coherence, a mode of regulation within them. It refers to the way in which these practices are constantly bound into ordered spaces and modalities of production and consumption, producing a variety of articulations of subjectivity distributed across and constitutive of a variety of audiences.

Secondly, it is by no means the case that each of the practices involved in this plurality has an equal social weight: the practices that constitute mainstream commercial cinema are massively dominant and therefore have a social presence and a social impact far in excess of any others. Indeed, not only do they provide the baseline in relation to which the others find their definition (as 'avant-garde', as 'political', as 'art', or whatever), but in doing so, they provide the terms and the examples in relation to which cinema itself—its forms and meanings, possibilities and pleasures—is both defined and understood.

Thirdly, regulation does not simply hinge upon mechanisms of repetition. Regulation is a *process*. Hence difference is a fundamental and a fundamentally active principle within each of the spheres of practice constitutive of cinema as a whole, including mainstream cinema. The very existence of distinct genres illustrates this point. Equally, however, difference is itself constantly regulated, and, as far as mainstream cinema is concerned, genres might be said to be the major instances of and instruments for such regulation.

The focus of the cinematic institution, of its industrial, commercial and

19

ideological practices, of the discourses that it circulates, is narrative. What mainstream cinema produces as its commodity is narrative cinema, cinema as narrative. Hence, at a general social level, the system of narration adopted by mainstream cinema serves as the very currency of cinema itself, defining the horizon of its aesthetic and ideological possibilities, providing the measure of cinematic 'literacy' and intelligibility. Hence, too, narrative is the primary instance and instrument of the regulatory processes that mark and define the ideological function of the cinematic institution as a whole.

Genre and Narrative

Narrative is always a process of transformation of the balance of elements that constitute its pretext: the interruption of an initial equilibrium and the tracing of the dispersal and refiguration of its components. The system of narration characteristic of mainstream cinema is one which orders that dispersal and refiguration in a particular way, so that dispersal, disequilibrium is both maintained and contained in figures of symmetry, of balance, its elements finally re-placed in a new equilibrium whose achievement is the condition of narrative closure.

Two points are important here. The first is that the 'elements' in question, their equilibrium and disequilibrium, their order/disorder, are not simply reducible to the signified components of a given narrative situation, nor are they solely the product of the narrative considered as a single discourse or discursive structure. Rather, they are signifiers articulated in a narrative process which is simultaneously that of the inscription of a number of discourses, and that of the modification, restructuration and transformation they each undergo as a result of their interaction. The second point, following on from this, is that equilibrium and disequilibrium, order and disorder are essentially a function of the relations of coherence between the discourses involved, of the compatibilities and contradictions that exist between them. Moreover, a definitive equilibrium, a condition of total plenitude, is always an impossibility. Disequilibrium, particularly in the form of dramatic conflict, is actually a means of containing that impossibility: it sutures* a lack which, if the equilibrium were to be simply maintained, would insist all the more strongly, all the more uncomfortably in the interstices of an ever more frenzied repetition.

Genres are modes of this narrative system, regulated orders of its potentiality. Hence it may be possible to begin here to indicate some of the elements of their specificity, some of the ways in which particular genres function simultaneously to exploit and contain the diversity of mainstream narrative. Firstly, it is necessary to consider the modes in which equilibrium and disruption are articulated, and the ways in which they are specified, represented differently and differen-

*In anatomy, suture refers to the stitching together of the lips of a wound in surgery. In psychoanalysis it refers to the juncture of the imaginary and the symbolic. For a further elaboration in this latter context see Stephen Heath, 'Notes on Suture', in *Screen*, Vol 18, no 4, Winter 1977/78 as well as the essays by J. A. Miller and J.-P. Oudart in the same issue.

tially, from genre to genre. In each case, the marks of generic specificity as such are produced by an articulation that is always constructed in terms of particular *combinations* of particular types or categories of discourse. The organisation of a given 'order' and of its disruption should be seen always in terms of conjunctions of and disjunctions between multiple sets of discursive categories and operations. For example, in the western, the gangster film and the detective film, disruption is always figured literally—as physical violence. Disequilibrium is inaugurated by violence which marks the process of the elements disrupted and which constitutes the means by which order is finally (re)established. In each case, equilibrium and disequilibrium are signified specifically in terms of Law, in terms of the presence/absence, effectiveness/ineffectiveness of legal institutions and their agents. In each case too, therefore, the discourses mobilised in these genres are discourses about crime, legality, justice, social order, civilisation, private property, civic responsibility and so on. Where they differ from one another is in the precise weight given to the discourses they share in common, in the inscription of these discourses across more specific generic elements, and in their imbrication across the codes specific to cinema. Of course, there are other genres which deploy figurations of violence. But the difference resides in the nature of the discourses and discursive categories employed in the specification of the order disrupted and the disorder instituted by that disruption.

For instance, violence also marks the horror film, most evidently in films where a monster—werewolf, vampire, psychopath or whatever—initiates a series of acts of murder and destruction which can only end when it itself is either destroyed or becomes normalised, i.e. becomes 'the norm', as in some of Polanski's films (*Rosemary's Baby, Dance of the Vampires*) or in Herzog's *Nosferatu.* But what defines the specificity of this particular genre is not the violence as such, but its conjunction with images and definitions of the monstrous. What defines its specificity with respect to the instances of order and disorder is their articulation across terms provided by categories and definitions of 'the human' and 'the natural'. The instances where the 'monster' is not destroyed but ends instead by pervading the social fabric in relation to which it functioned as 'monster', thus becoming integrated into it, becoming normalised, constitute a special option for the horror genre, testifying to the relative weight of discourses carrying the human/nature opposition in its discursive regime, relativising or even displacing entirely the Law/disorder dichotomy in terms of which violence operates in the western, the detective and gangster films. The monster, and the disorder it initiates and concretises, is always that which disrupts and challenges the definitions and categories of the 'human' and the 'natural'. Generally speaking, it is the monster's body which focuses the disruption. Either disfigured, or marked by a heterogeneity of human and animal features, or marked only by a 'non-human' gaze, the body is always in some way signalled as 'other', signalled, precisely, as monstrous. A variant on this is the inscription of a disruption in the spatio-temporal scales governing the order of the 'human' and of 'nature', producing figures such as giants—be they animals or humans—or, alternatively, homunculi, dwarfs, and so on. In other words, the order involved here is explicitly metaphysical. Moreover, narrative disruption and disequilibrium are specified overtly in terms of discursive disjunctions between 'the empirical' ('the real') and 'the supernatural' ('the unnatural'), as well as between the concatenation of diegetic events and the discourses and discursive categories used by the characters (and, often, the audience) to understand them. *Psycho* is a perfect case in point. The events that occur are 'explained' in a way which upsets conventional categories of character motivation and sexual identity, although in this instance the 'metaphysics' are given a 'scientific' rather than a religious character. The latter tends to predominate in the gothic horror film—such as *Dracula*, or *Frankenstein*—where 'unnatural' acts of brutality and destruction, 'impossible' metamorphoses of identity, 'supernatural' happenings of all kinds, defy the principles both of common sense and of science—at least as these are defined in the films. Hence the narrative process in the horror films tends to be marked by a search for that discourse, that specialised form of knowledge which will enable the human characters to comprehend and to control that which simultaneously embodies and causes its 'trouble'. The function of characters such as the psychiatrist in *Psycho* or Van Helsing in the *Dracula* films is precisely to introduce and to articulate such a discourse.

In the musical and the melodrama, violence may figure in an important way, as it does for instance in *West Side Story* or *Written on the Wind*, but it is not a defining characteristic as such, either in terms of the register of disruption or in terms of its diegetic specification. In both genres the narrative process is inaugurated by the eruption of (hetero)sexual desire into an already firmly established social order. That is to say, the discourse of the law and 'criminality' is marginalised although by no means eliminated, while the metaphysical discourse of the horror genre is either refused entirely or explicitly designated as phantasy. The role of the policeman in *West Side Story* and that of the court in *Written on the Wind*, when compared to the roles these agencies of the legal apparatus play in *Anatomy of a Murder* (each in its own way a family romance), illustrate the difference in status of the legal discourse in the different genres. In the melodrama and the musical, the eruption of sexuality is not inscribed primarily across the codes of legality, as it can be in the thriller or the detective genre, and even, occasionally, in the western (e.g. *Stagecoach*). On the contrary, the disequilibrium inaugurating the narrative movement is specified as the process of desire itself and of the various blockages to its fulfilment within an apparently 'common sense', established social order. In other words, the process of desire in melodrama interrupts or problematises precisely the order the discourse and actions of the law have established in the face of 'lawlessness' and social disorder. Melodrama thus puts into crisis the discourses within the domain circumscribed by and defined as the legally established social order, the kind of order instituted at the end of westerns and detective films. Melodrama does not suggest a crisis of that order, but a crisis within it, an 'in house' rearrangement.

In short, it should be clearly understood that in each example mentioned here, I am not referring to elements which, in and of themselves, are absolutely exclusive to particular genres. Generic specificity is a question not of particular and exclusive elements, however defined, but of exclusive and particular combinations and articulations of elements, of the exclusive and particular weight given in any one genre to elements which in fact it shares with other genres. Heterosexual desire, the element mentioned here, is of course by no means exclusive to the musical or to the melodrama. But the role it plays in these genres is specific and distinctive. Not only does it have a much greater functional role in the generation of the narrative, not only does it provide the motivation for the actions of the principal characters, it also occupies a central as opposed to a secondary or peripheral place in the discursive ensemble mobilised and shaped by these particular genres. In short, its presence is a necessity, not a variable option.

In the musical, desire and satisfaction are generally signified in terms of two sets of discursive oppositions: firstly, that between the private and the public, and secondly, that between social success and failure. Each of these two sets is then articulated across a scale whose polar instances are harmony on the one hand and discord on the other.

Harmony and discord are terms used to specify aspects of equilibrium and disequilibrium in music. In this context, they are used to suggest that it is the specific inscription of music as the determining principle in the arrangement of sound-image relations as well as of relations between elements within the image that distinguishes the genre as such. It is the specific inscription of music into the plurality of discourses that constitute the text which ultimately shapes, determines and marks the register in which equilibrium and disequilibrium achieve their most intense expression and in which narrative resolution finally occurs. In other words, sequences of song and dance represent a shift in the regime of the narrative discourse, marked, for example, by a different articulation of body and voice. These sequences, this 'other' regime, woven into the narrative, allow a particularly intense and coherent statement of the conflicts, tensions and problems that traverse the narrative as a whole. They also, at certain points in some musical films, represent the terms of a resolution to these conflicts, tensions and problems; in the 'Dancing in the Dark' sequence in *The Bandwagon*, the fact that Cyd Charisse and Fred Astaire dance together so perfectly indicates that their initial hostility to one another will be and to a large extent already has been resolved in terms of a rhythmical interaction of their bodies. Whether such a resolution occurs in all song and dance sequences or not, the point here is that these musically determined sequences, in their completion and perfection, represent the discursive mode in relation to which resolution or lack of resolution are to be measured and through which stability and equilibrium are ultimately to be achieved.

Of course, the body and the voice are not the only elements involved here— decor, colour, dress, camera movement, editing and so on are all involved; all are transformed and integrated, all are subject to an explicitly aesthetic form of organisation in so far as it is music which governs the arrangement of signifying relations between and within images as well as between image and sound. This may be why the musical has come to be regarded as the most 'stylised', the most 'aestheticised' of genres, and why it is marked by the constant presence of discourses on art, entertainment and show business.

Finally, the different forms of comedy work by specifying disruption in relation to discourse itself. Crazy comedy tends to articulate order and disorder across the very mechanisms of discourse, producing incongruities, contradictions and illogicalities at the level of language and code, while social (situation) comedy, on the other hand, tends to specify its disorder as the disturbance of socially institutionalised discursive hierarchies. It is important to stress that these two forms are indeed only tendencies. There are overt social implications in much of the comedy of Chaplin, the Marx Brothers, Tashlin and Hawks, just as there are frequent instances of a play with the logical mechanisms of discourse in Lubitsch, Capra and Sturges. But nevertheless the two types of comedy remain distinct as specific emphases and tendencies.

Paul Willemen has pointed to the mode of operation of crazy comedy in his discussion of the workings of the gags in Tashlin's cinema. He stresses in particular the extent to which these gags are dependent upon specifically semiotic sets of logic, the extent to which they function by treating the elements in a situation as units of a language:

'. . . there are a great number of gags based on variations of the basic forms of combination. If we accept that the basic forms of combination consist of the bringing together of two or more items to produce a new structure, then a variation is constituted by such gags as the baby getting lost in the powder in *Rock-A-Bye-Baby* or the man in a plaster cast disappearing in *The Disorderly Orderly*. The plaster cast gag is not merely a form of subtraction, because the viewer is not supposed to consider the unfortunate invalid as a composite of parts of equal value—plaster cast plus man. In the same way, neither is a powdered baby regarded as a combination of two elements of equal value, either of which can be withdrawn from the equation—the baby without the powder/the powder without the baby. In this way, Tashlin's gags of this kind literally deconstruct, disassemble visual/semantic units.'[2]

At the purely verbal level, where mechanisms of this kind are at their most overt as operations of discourse, one could point to a number of examples in the Marx Brothers films, where dialogue follows a logic of its own, thus leading to semantic and dramatic absurdities: 'I know where the suspects are: they're in the house next door'—'But there isn't any house next door'—'Then we build a house next door'. As detectives in *Animal Crackers,* they reason their way from 'This portrait was painted by a left-handed painter' to 'This picture was eaten by a left-handed moth'.

Many of Chaplin's gags, to return to the situation level, are dependent upon a mixing of the registers of behaviour and action. The meal of boots in *The Gold Rush* is a classic example, as is the making of the bed in a water-filled trench in *Shoulder Arms*. Both depend upon a logic in which behaviour is both logical and illogical, both appropriate and inappropriate given the situation in which it takes place. In both instances, however, there are also overt 'social' implications to the gags and to the structure upon which they depend.

Social comedy proper proceeds by mapping the field of a socio-discursive order, a field whose nodal points tend constantly to be those of class and sexu-

24

ality. The order is disturbed in order for its hierarchy to be re-arranged. The establishment of a new, 'better' hierarchy is the condition of narrative closure. Capra's films are particularly clear examples. Thus both in *Mr. Smith Goes to Washington* and in *Mr. Deeds Goes to Town* the initial narrative equilibrium is specified in markedly 'social' terms (in *Mr. Smith* it concerns political institutions and is centred on the Senate; in *Mr. Deeds* it concerns wealth, particularly as centred in and distributed by financial institutions). That equilibrium, centred in each case in the city, is presented as both corrupt and unjust and yet as normative within its milieu. A naive, 'idealistic' character comes from outside and operates, in narrative terms, to re-order the initial elements so that the final equilibrium is different, and to focus that re-ordering as ethically necessary. The outsider is the bearer of a discourse which, in its contrast with the city discourses, produces humour and comedy, and which in its principles articulates the terms in relation to which the final equilibrium is to be measured.

Genre, Narrative and Subject

Narrative is not simply a product or a structure, nor even a process of production, an activity of structuration. It is both a process of production and an activity of structuration, but it is so in and for a subject. The subject is a function, or better, a functioning of signification. Different modes of signification produce different functionings of subjectivity, moving the subject differently in their various semiotic processes, producing distinct modes of address. Mainstream narrative is a mode of signification which works constantly to produce coherence in the subject through and across the heterogeneity of the effects that it mobilises and structures. Specifying its effects as narrative functions, pulling those functions into figures of symmetry and balance, mainstream narrative binds together, implicating the subject as the point where its binding mechanisms cohere, the point from where the deployment and configuration of discourses makes 'sense'. The subject thus is 'carried through against the dispersion, the multiple intensities of the text of the film'.[3]

Coherence, therefore, is not simply a fact of closure, of the achievement of the stability of an equilibrium, of the production of a final unified position. It is also and equally a fact of the process which leads to that closure, of the balance of the movement of positioning that disequilibrium itself involves. Its operation is complex and multiple rather than simple and single. Narrative disruption, for example, does not involve the disturbance of one subject position as such, but rather the disturbance of a set of positions, the production of a disphasure in the relations between a plurality of positions inscribed in a plurality of discourses.[4] The coherence of mainstream narrative derives largely from the way in which that disphasure is contained as a series of oscillations that never exceed the limits of 'dramatic conflict' (that never, therefore, exceed the limits of the possibility of resolution), and from the way in which such conflict is always, ultimately, articulated from a single, privileged point of view.

Fundamental, then, to the economy of the subject in mainstream narrative, to the economy of its mode of address, is the achievement of the maintenance

25

of a coherent balance between process (enunciation) on the one hand, and position (enounced) on the other. But this economy can be structured in a variety of ways. Genres represent systematisations of that variety. Each genre has, to some extent at least, its own system of narrative address, its own version of the articulation of the balance. Each genre also, therefore, engages and structures differently the two basic subjective mechanisms which any form of the balance involves: the want for the pleasure of process, and the want for the pleasure of its closure.

For example, consider the detective film and the characteristic mode of its narrative address, suspense. Suspense is not, of course, exclusive to the detective genre, but it is nonetheless essential to it, tying in as it does with a narrative structured around the investigation of the principle of narrative disorder itself in the sense that the enigma is a mystery, an 'incoherence' functioning as the trigger for a story, which, as it unfolds, eliminates the enigma and comes to an end when its disorder has been abolished. The narrative of the detective genre thus directly dramatises the tension inherent in the signifying process through the mobilisation of a series of discourses concerned specifically with the Law, with the symbolic and with knowledge. What the enigma-investigation structure serves to effect is an amplification of the tension inherent in all 'classic' narratives: the tension between process (with its threat of incoherence, of the loss of mastery) and position (with its threat of stasis, fixity or of compulsive repetition, which is the same thing in another form). This tension, which informs all semiotic systems in so far as they are grounded in desire, realises itself in two distinct forms of pleasure: firstly, the potential 'boredom' of stasis; and, secondly, pleasure in position in the face of the anxieties potentially attendant on unlimited process. The amplification of this tension is largely due to the fact that the detective film dramatises the signification process itself as its fundamental problem: the Law is at issue directly in the investigation, that is to say, in the play between two fluctuatingly related sets of knowledge, that of the detective and that of the audience. In the detective film, the detective *and* the audience have to make sense of a set of disparate events, signs and clues. The 'risk' for the detective being represented in the narrative is a risk of violence and death. The risk for the audience is a loss of sense and meaning, the loss of a position of mastery. On the other hand, though, for the audience the process of the narrative is the primary source of its pleasure. The viewing subject is thus suspended in a structure which stretches the tensions of classic narrative to breaking point though never, axiomatically, beyond it.

There is an important dimension to suspense, and indeed to narrative address in general, which, again, the detective film illustrates particularly well. Narrative is always and essentially a means of organising and articulating process, of organising and articulating both the temporal flow of the text, and the flow, the fluctuation óf the subject within it. In the words of Stephen Heath, narrative is thus always and essentially

'a system which, positioning and effecting, is a ceaseless performance of the subject in time for the reality given, of subject-time. The performance of

26

subject-time is itself a complex time, phasing between two constant moments that—these remarks concern classic narrative cinema, the commercial exploitation of film—are layered together: the subject-reflection and subject-process (the layering and balance of the two being the film's performance of subject-time). The subject-reflection is a narrative effect (or series of effects): in the movement of the chain of differences—the flow of multiple intensities of image and sound—the narrative defines terms for the movements of the chain, specifies relations and reflects a subject as the direction of those relations, produces the coherence of view and viewer. Going along with the subject-reflection, the subject-process is just that: the process all the elements of the system in its production-performance, the whole apparatus of the representation; a multiple circulation, the perpetual movement of difference. . .'[5]

Mainstream narrative regulates complexly the times of its semiotic processes by balancing, on the one hand, points of advance in ceaselessly pushing the flow of text and subject forward, and, on the other hand, points of recall in ceaselessly containing that process in figures of repetition, folding it back on itself into the retrospective coherence of memory. But it can do so in a variety of ways, through a variety of modes of address institutionalised in a variety of genres.

Returning to the detective film, the function of the enigma is to structure the generation of suspense, but it achieves this not simply by articulating the narrative as a puzzle, but also by specifying the puzzle in particular temporal terms. The enigma focuses two initially separate times, the past time of the story behind the crime and the present time of its reconstruction.[6] Indeed the enigma in many ways is that separation of times. Eventually, the two times are brought together coherently and the enigma is resolved. A coherent memory is thus constructed across the separate instances of the story of the crime, the story of its investigation, and the process of the text itself: the memory constructed within the film duplicates the memory constructed by the film. This temporal duplication, the creation of a double temporal tension, is precisely that which marks and generates the tension referred to earlier. It is therefore also that which marks and generates its suspense, the temporal dimension of which has been outlined by Barthes as follows:

'On meeting in "life", it is most unlikely that the invitation to take a seat would not immediately be followed by the act of sitting down; in narrative these two units, contiguous from a mimetic point of view, may also be separated by a long series of insertions belonging to quite different functional spheres. Thus is established a kind of logical time which has very little connection with real time, the apparent pulverization of units always being firmly held in place by the logic that binds together the nuclei of the sequence. Suspense is clearly only a privileged—or exacerbated—form of distortion: on the one hand, by keeping a sequence open (through emphatic procedures of delay and renewal), it reinforces the contact with the reader (the listener), has a manifestly phatic function; while on the other, it offers the threat of an uncomplicated sequence, of an open paradigm (if, as we believe, every sequence has two poles), that is to say, of a logical disturbance, it being this disturbance which is consumed with anxiety and pleasure (all the more so because it is always made right in the end).'[7]

This point, apparently so banal, is in fact fundamental not only for understanding the economy of pleasure in the mainstream text, but also for understanding the function of genres themselves: genres institutionalise, guarantee coherence by institutionalising conventions, i.e. sets of expectations with respect to narrative process and narrative closure which may be subject to variation, but which are never exceeded or broken. The existence of genres means that the spectator, precisely, will always know that everything will be 'made right in the end', that everything will cohere, that any threat or any danger in the narrative process itself will always be contained.

Suspense is equally as powerful and equally as characteristic, with respect to generic address, both in the gangster film and in the thriller. These genres, however, inscribe their suspense differently, through different narrative structures and in conjunction with different diegetic conventions. Suspense in the gangster film derives from an amplification of the tensions of narration, not by augmenting the threat of incoherence through the constitution of the narrative as a puzzle, nor by specifying that tension across a temporal axis of past and present. Instead, it is achieved, firstly, by identifying the necessity for the existence of the narrative with the existence of the gangsters' activities while identifying the necessity for narrative closure with the existence of the Law. In the gangster film, of course, the Law tends to be specified in terms of a particular, datable, historical law, such as prohibition. The Law in the detective film is less specific, coming often to function as the signifier of symbolic Law itself. The pleasures and anxieties of position are thus made more complex by being articulated across an ideological division between the legal and the illegal. Since the former provides the grounds for a primary identification with the narrative as such, and since the latter provides the grounds for secondary forms of identification, a series of potential gaps and contradictions opens up, across which narrative and subject are suspended. Secondly, suspense is achieved by structuring the narrative across an axis of present and future. One of the major activities in which the gangsters engage is planning—the planning of robberies, assassinations, vendettas, and so on, of activities which will serve to sustain and increase individual as well as corporate wealth and power. The narrative and its subject are thus constantly anticipating. It is the play with this anticipation, the tension in the potential or actual difference between what is planned and what occurs, which provides a major means by which suspense is engendered and articulated in the gangster film, both at the micro-narrative level (the level of scene or segment) and at the level of the structure of the narrative as a whole.

Suspense involves a particular form of affect, what Barthes has called a 'thrilling of intelligibility',[8] and it is to this form that the generic label 'thriller' refers. The thriller in fact may involve a variety of narrative structures and may create its suspense in various ways. It may borrow elements from the detective film: the positing of an enigma—Hitchcock's McGuffin—and the use of an investigative structure; or it may borrow from the gangster film, playing off identification and pleasure by focusing much of the narrative on the activities of a criminal protagonist; or it may use elements and structures of its own. One of the commonest of these involves the playing of its protagonist in a position such that he (or, occasionally, she) is under threat both from a set of criminals and from the Law. Examples here would include Lang's *Woman in the Window*, Sirk's *Shockproof* and, of course, many of Hitchcock's films–*Strangers on a Train, The Thirty Nine Steps, North by Northwest* and so on. This increases not only the danger to the protagonist, but also the number and complexity of the tasks that have to be performed if all the ends of the story are to be brought together coherently, if the narrative is to end 'satisfactorily'. Thus the wish for the narrative to continue is articulated across the fact that this involves a considerable number of risks, while the wish for it to end is articulated across the fact that the complexity of the situation in which the protagonist finds himself has fully to be worked out. Whatever the structure, whatever the specificity of the diegesis in any particular thriller, the genre as a whole, unlike that of the gangster or the detective story, is specified in the first instance by its address, by the fact that it always, though in different ways, must have the generation of suspense as its core strategy.

Other genres are marked by other modes of narrative address, other ways of articulating the two 'wants' of narrative, suspending the subject in other structures of affect. In comedy, for instance, the mode of affect is laughter, a release of pleasure which comes from a structuring of the two narrative wants and pleasures across the point of intersection of two (or more) discourses, of two (or more) discursive structures or regimes, together with the economy, the appropriateness–the wit–with which the contradictions and resistances generated between them are overcome. This may occur firstly through a 'triumph' over that which is represented to be resisting, as, for example, in many of Buster Keaton's films, where what is signified as resisting is often, simply, 'reality'. Here laughter comes not only from the overcoming of the resistance, but also, and primarily, from the fact that that overcoming involves a drastic (but coherent) re-ordering of the logic of the discourses which, together, define the field and order of 'reality' in the film concerned. Alternatively, and secondly, it may come about through the 'triumph' of that which resists (as, for example, in a banana peel gag). Laughter here stems in particular from the way in which an anticipation of the inevitable is played across the specific temporal articulation of the event anticipated, from, precisely, the timing of the gag, joke or comic scene, the temporal–and logical–economy with which it is structured and realised, the suspense it embodies. Excellent examples of this type of comedy where gags are as it were telegraphed in advance but achieve their effect exclusively through timing, through the variations of the 'delay' between cause and effect, are to be found in Blake Edwards' work, and particularly in the *Pink Panther* series. The particularity of the address of melodrama derives from an articulation of the mechanisms of the suspense basic to any narrative across a representation of the vicissitudes of (hetero)sexual desire as they, in turn, articulate with a series of discourses about class, sexuality, property and the family. The representation of desire itself engages 'directly', so to speak, the twin pleasures of narrative by giving them representation in

29

terms of (a specific version) of desire itself. The tension between them is thereby heightened, since the wish for the narrative to continue is structured as directly in conflict with a wish for the representation of fulfilment of desire, while the wish for the narrative to end coherently is organised in conflict with a pleasure in the process of desire itself. The articulation thus produced is responsible for the particular poignancy with which the melodrama as a genre is associated, irrespective of whether any individual melodrama has a 'happy' ending or a 'sad' one. This because there is, in fact, always an experience of loss involved in the *mise en scène* of desire, stemming from the nature of desire itself, in that temporally and structurally its very existence is a function of lack.

Finally, the musical, though not perhaps associated with any particular mode of affect, has a particular form of address which stems from its balance of narrative and spectacle. As Patricia Mellencamp has noted,[9] moments of spectacle, generally in the form of singing and dancing, are always separated off, to some degree at least, from the linear flow of the story. These moments are moments of intense gratification and pleasure, realising the desire for coherence and process simultaneously in a harmony of bodily movement, voice, music and *mise en scène.* They tend to occur in particular at points of stress (whether for the characters, the narrative or the subject and its pleasures and desires), thus contributing towards an economy which in many ways is the antithesis of that of the genres of suspense: 'These breaks [in the narrative, instances of spectacle] displace the temporal advance of the narrative, providing immediate, regular doses of gratification rather than delaying the pleasures until The End.'[10]

Spectacle itself, however, cannot be sustained for any length of time without variation (otherwise the lack at the base of its apparent plenitude would begin to insist, thus disturbing the gratification). Hence the necessity, as far as mainstream cinema is concerned, for the narrative to return in order to provide that variation in a time that extends beyond that of the 'spectacular moment' itself. Therefore, rather than the two being in conflict, with spectacle 'subverting' narrative, as Mellencamp tends to argue, they in fact function to reinforce and support each other, the 'deficiencies' of the one being minimised by the 'virtues' of the other, and vice-versa. Moreover, in providing two registers of discourse within the overall coherence of a contained textual system, the musical doubles the possibilities of its semiotic effects while simultaneously doubling the forms of their coherence. Doubling the play of its desires and pleasures, it simultaneously doubles the modes of their binding together.

Genre and Cinema

The cinematic institution exists predominantly to produce narrative, cinema as narrative, but equally, and thereby defining its place within the social formation as a whole, it exists to produce narrative as cinema. The regime of meaning and pleasure, the discursive order specific to the mode of narrative it employs, is produced in conjunction with the regimes of meaning and pleasure specific to cinema: narrative produced as cinematic narrative, through the matters of expression and the codes specific to cinema that historically have become institutionalised.

Cinema includes all the facilities of sound and of the moving photographic image. These together form the basis of its specificity as a signifying medium. The codes of cinema (codes of editing, camera movement, spatio-temporal configuration) exist to order those facilities, and, in mainstream cinema, both are subordinate to, regulated by, narrative. Thus, for instance, movement is contained as narrative continuity and space as narrative scene: 'Filmic procedures are to be held as narrative instances (very much as "cues"), exhaustively, without gap or contradiction.' (Stephen Heath).[11] Cinema, then, is contained as narrative. But the term to stress here is 'contain': there is no question either of effacement or of transparency: 'It is too readily assumed that the operation—the determination, the effect, the pleasure—of classical cinema lies in the attempt at an invisibility of process, the intended transparency of a kind of absolute "realism" from which all signs of production have been effaced. The actual case is much more complex and subtle, and much more telling. Classical cinema does not efface the signs of production, it contains them.' (Stephen Heath).[12]

Moreover, such containment can and does allow for (regulated) forms of excess, and (regulated) forms of the display of its process: part of the very function of genres is precisely to display a variety of the possibilities of the semiotic processes of mainstream narrative cinema while simultaneously containing them as genre. Hence the musical 'with its systematic "freedom" of space—crane, choreography—and its shifting balances of narrative and spectacle . . .';[13] or the film noir, with its display of the possibilities of chiaroscuro lighting, frequently unmotivated, diegetically impossible; or the epic, with all the resources of cinema in terms of widescreen, decor, colour, costume and so on invested in a spectacle which at many points simply goes beyond its strictly narrative function; or the science fiction film, where, from a certain perspective, the narrative functions largely to motivate the production of special effects, climaxing either with the 'best' of those effects (*Close Encounters of the Third Kind*), or with the point at which they are multiplied with greatest intensity (*Star Wars*).

The problem of cinematic specificity, beyond its definition in terms of particular matters of expression and the codes that traverse them, also poses the question as to what kind of subject it constructs, what kind of subjective mechanisms it engages and the way in which it organises them. Cinematic specificity is therefore, above all, a question as to the nature of what Christian Metz has termed 'the cinematic signifier':

'It is indeed well known that different "languages" (painting, music, cinema, etc.) are distinguished from one another—and are first several—by means of their signifiers, in the physical and perceptual definitions of those signifiers as well as in the formal and structural features that flow from them, and not by means of their signifieds, or at any rate, not immediately . . . There is no signified which is peculiar to literature or on the contrary to cinema, no "great global signified" that might be attributed to painting itself, for

31

example (= one more mythical avatar of the belief in the ultimate signified). Each means of expression allows everything to be said: by "everything" I mean an indefinite number of things, broadly coinciding from one language to another. Obviously each one says them in its own way, and that is precisely why it sometimes seems that there should be such a great signified. But a signified which is still very badly named, since it can only be approached in terms of a signifier: the cinematic does not consist of some static list of themes or subjects which are supposed to be especially apt for the cinema and for which the other arts have a lesser "vocation" (a truly metaphysical conception, proceeding by essences), it can only be defined, or rather foreseen, as a special way of saying anything (or nothing), i.e. as a signifier effect: a specific coefficient of signification (and not a signified) linked to the intrinsic workings of the cinema and to its very adoption rather than that of another machine, another apparatus.'[14]

Following the passage quoted here, Metz goes on to indicate some of the properties of the cinematic signifier, and to specify some of their effects, in terms of the subject relations they institute and structure, that is to say, in terms of the spectating subject they inscribe. It is worth outlining some of these properties and effects, especially in the forms in which they have been institutionalised in mainstream cinema, in order to relate them to the functioning of the cinematic genres and to their respective specificities. The basic characteristic of the cinematic signifier is its fundamentally 'fictional' status. Like theatre and opera, cinema engages a large number of perceptual registers. But unlike them, the various perceptual mechanisms centre around objects which are not in themselves physically present:

'The actor, the "decor", the words one hears are all absent, everything is recorded (as a memory trace which is immediately so, without having been something else before), and this is still true if what is recorded is not a "story" and does not aim for the fictional illusion proper, for it is the signifier itself, and as a whole, that is recorded, that is absence.'[15]

As such, the cinematic signifier is 'closer to fantasy at the onset', engaging the imaginary in an especially profound and forceful way:

'Thus the cinema, "more perceptual" than certain arts according to the lists of its sensory registers, is also "less perceptual" than others once the status of these perceptions is envisaged rather than their number or diversity: for its perceptions are all in a sense false. Or rather, the activity of perception in it is real (the cinema is not a fantasy), but the perceived is not really an object, it is its shade, its phantom, its double, its replica in a new kind of mirror . . . The unique position of the cinema lies in this dual character of its signifier: unaccustomed perceptual wealth, but unusually profoundly stamped with unreality, from its very beginning. More than the other arts, or in a more unique way, the cinema involves us in the imaginary: it drums up all perception, but to switch it immediately over into its own absence, which is nonetheless the only signifier present.'[16]

Hence the double simultaneous emotional investment in cinema, firstly, as the trace and the mirror (the guarantee) of reality, i.e. of the number, diversity and density of perceptual registers deployed; and, secondly, as one of the primary vehicles of narrative fiction, defined as the correlation between the 'fictional' aspect of the cinematic signifier and the fictions it is used to construct. This double investment undermines not only the fictional narratives characterised by the wholesale adoption of the conventions of 'realism', it also programmes, to some extent at least, the fantasies of critics such as Bazin in search of the elusive (because impossible) synthesis of one with the other.

The double investment required and solicited by cinema has certain consequences for the spectating subject constructed by the cinematic institution: the fundamental implication of quite specific modes of scopophilia, exhibitionism and fetishism. Scopophilia, a drive which has the look as its object of desire, is evidently of crucial importance to the cinema. It is a drive that is dependent upon the maintenance of a distance between subject and object, and, as Metz notes, drives of this kind are characteristic of most of the 'major' arts. What distinguishes cinema from other arts such as theatre or opera is that distance is inscribed into its very signifier: all its objects are always already absent, present only as recorded traces: 'Not only am I at a distance from the object, as in the theatre, but what remains in that distance is no longer the object itself, it is a delegate it has sent me while itself withdrawing. A double withdrawal.' (C. Metz)[17] The implication of this 'double withdrawal' is, firstly, an intensifying of the scopic drive—hence the whole battery of devices and strategies for soliciting and containing scopophilia in mainstream narrative film, most notably, perhaps, the relay of 'looks' that it sets in play,[18] each working ultimately to satisfy, to afford pleasure, rather than to expose the subject in the gap, the 'want' founding scopophilia, like any other form of desire. The second implication, reinforcing the first, is that the aspect of exhibitionism in the object looked at, i.e. in the film itself, appears to be weakened:

'What defines the specifically cinematic scopic regime is not so much the distance kept, the "keeping" itself (first figure of the lack, common to all voyeurism), as the absence of the object seen. Here the cinema is profoundly different from the theatre as also from more intimate voyeuristic activities with a specifically erotic aim (there are intermediate genres, moreover: certain cabaret acts, striptease, etc.): cases where voyeurism remains linked to exhibitionism, where the two faces, active and passive, of the component drive are by no means so dissociated; where the object seen is present and hence presumably complicit . . .'[19]

The subject is thus all the more invisible, inscribed as 'unauthorised' voyeur by the film (of course, voyeurism is 'authorised' by the institution as a whole), and the instance of scopophilia involved 'is from the outset more strongly established than that of the theatre'. Metz goes on to point out that in this way, the scopophilia involved in the experience of watching a film is intimately related to the inscription of a viewer-voyeur in the primal scene phantasy (the phantasy scene of watching parents making love). Moreover, the affinity between these two phantasy spectacles is reinforced, firstly by the arrangement of the apparatus of exhibition: 'The obscurity surrounding the onlooker, the aperture of the screen with its inevitable keyhole effect'; and secondly, by the nature of what is exhibited: 'The filmic spectacle, the object seen, is more radically ignorant of its spectator, since he is not there, than the theatrical spectator ever can be.'[20] The film is then 'something that lets itself be seen without presenting itself to be seen, which has gone out of the room before leaving only its trace visible there'.[21] The arrangement is reinforced by the way mainstream narrative organises its discourses, suppressing all the marks of the subject of enunciation wherever possible. 'The film is not exhibitionist. I look at it, but it does not look at me looking at it.'[22] Exhibitionism appears to be weakened. However, as Metz himself notes, it is far from absent. It cannot be, because cinema depends on voyeurism, and voyeurism is inseparable from exhibitionism. Both must always exist together, and to precisely the same degree. Hence all those strategies of mainstream cinema for soliciting the look: 'eye-catching' compositions, sets and costumes, the putting on display of stars and décor and forms of movement and action. This is not to contradict Metz' statements, merely to modify them: what happens in mainstream cinema is that the instances of voyeurism and exhibitionism are constantly dislocated, the latter, for example, constantly diegeticised, contained within the films which appear to unreel, unsolicited, before the eyes of the spectator. Nonetheless the modification needs to be made, because if the 'subject or enunciation' is taken to be the cinematic institution itself, its marks are not absented but in fact pervade mainstream narrative films, since films are there precisely to exhibit cinema. Consider, for example, all the elements that can be grouped together under the heading of 'production values'—sets, costumes, locations, stars, special effects, expensive camera movements and so on. All these are marks of the cinematic institution and are displayed to the spectator as such.

It should also be noted here that the institution not only renews itself through the introduction and modification (updating) of such elements—sound, colour and widescreens are only the most spectacular instances—but also that such renewal takes place through the mechanisms of institutionalised exhibitionism mentioned earlier. What should be noted too, and this is important for my subsequent argument, is that this process takes place through conventionally institutionalised forms of which genre is one of the most important. For instance, the introduction of sound is displayed as and through the musical; widescreen is introduced and displayed as and through the epic; more recently, a sophisticated technology of special effects and sound are introduced and displayed as and through a genre: science fiction (*Star Wars* and *Close Encounters of the Third Kind*).

This means that genres also exhibit cinema, with different genres functioning to exhibit different aspects of its potentiality, each of them modulating instances of scopophilia and exhibitionism in different ways. And while it is not, I think, the case that each genre can be defined as systematically modulating and engaging particular versions of these instances, it is the case that genres

34

such as the musical and the epic are conventionally held to be distinct from most of the others in respect of the degree of spectacle they involve.

The discursive instances in these genres to which the term 'spectacle' is generally applied are clearly instances of overt exhibitionism, diegetically motivated it is true, but often precisely by narrative actions in which exhibitionism plays an especially powerful and evident role. For example, theatre and cabaret, referred to by Metz as forms of entertainment in which exhibitionism is marked both through the presence of the subject/object on display and through the conventions structuring that presentation, are often essential ingredients of the diegesis of the musical. The musical's moments of spectacle and display are often moments of theatre (think, for instance, of the Busby Berkeley musicals or of the prevalent motif of 'putting on a show'). Cinema always exceeds theatre in such moments. That is the whole point—cinema inscribes theatre in order to demonstrate its superiority over theatre. But it does so in a controlled manner, the element of control stemming precisely from the initial diegetic motivation. Cinema never exceeds too much. Its exhibitionism is controlled, limited, just enough to entertain and impress the spectator, to satisfy and to legitimate his or her voyeurism.

Elements of theatre and 'cabaret' are also prevalent in the epic, as are entertainments that are specific to the genre—chariot races, gladiatorial combats and so on. The epic is also marked by other instances of spectacle such as parades, ceremonies and marches, instances which are motivated quite specifically as displays of power. In this way, the epic explicitly mobilises and thematises the sadistic and masochistic components of scopophilia and exhibitionism, both of which thus reflect and actively articulate the theme of power that characterises the genre as a whole. The former instances of entertainment—the chariot races and combats, displays of physical power and/or strength, are also involved here, since they always take place in a narrative context in which they are subject to the controlling gaze of a representative or representatives of whatever Ancient State Power happens to be the focus of the discursive representation in any particular epic film.

Of course, spectacle in these genres is not confined to their moments of diegetic exhibitionism, but such moments are indicative both of the degree of exhibitionism involved in the epic and in the musical, and, hence, of the specific modalities of spectacle that they each inscribe in their own way. In the epic, these moments are part of an overall process in which cinema displays itself and its powers through the re-creation of a past so distant that much of its impact derives simply from the evidence of the scale of re-creation involved (from details of costume and decor to the construction of whole cities) and through the telling of a story felt to match that scale, such as the story of Christ, the fall of the Roman Empire, and so on. In the musical, on the other hand, cinema is engaged in the production of spectacle as spectacle, in the demonstration of its own codes of signification in accordance with its own ideology of art. It is this demonstration which motivates and controls the degree to which those codes are displayed in the process of construction of art itself (singing and dancing, putting on a show), and the degree to which discourses about art and entertainment are central to the genre.

Fetishism

Fetishism is a psychic structure which psychoanalysis has shown to be founded upon the disavowal of sexual difference. As such, it 'turns' on the privileged signifier of that difference (presence/absence of the phallus) and characteristically involves a 'splitting of belief' as in the phrase: 'I know very well this is so, and yet . . .' Cinema activates fetishistic structures in a number of ways. Firstly, the cinematic signifier itself is such that it initiates an oscillation in the 'regime of credence' which it provokes or allows. The cinematic signifier is perceptually present, but it nevertheless exists as a trace of absence. As Metz put it: 'The actor, the decor, the words one hears are all absent, everything is recorded . . . it is the signifier itself . . . that is recorded, that is absence.'[15] As such, the very status of the cinematic signifier inaugurates a 'splitting of belief', the regime of credence that can be characterised as 'I know very well, and yet . . .' (I know this is only cinema, and yet it is so 'present' . . .). Of course, there are other aspects of cinema, particularly of narrative-figurative cinema, which implicate viewers in fetishistic structures such as the use of stars' faces, representations of the female figure, uses of dress, etc. These aspects of cinema have been examined by Laura Mulvey and Danièle Dubroux, among others.[23] In this context, the main point to note is that fetishism is a structure involving the production of regimes of credence and as such has a part to play in the 'reality effect' of cinema as well as in the establishing of the conventions of verisimilitude. Metz made the provision that

> 'the precise nuance of the regime of credence that the spectator will adopt varies tolerably from one fictional technique to another. In the cinema, as in the theatre, the represented is by definition imaginary; that is what characterises fiction as such, independently of the signifier in charge of it. But the representation is fully real in the theatre, whereas in the cinema it too is imaginary, the material being already a reflection'.[24]

In mainstream narrative cinema, intent on the production of the viewer's adherence to a coherent and homogeneous diegesis, the fetishism of the signifier becomes further implicated in the fetishism of fiction itself:

> 'The audience is not duped by the diegetic illusion, it "knows" that the screen presents no more than a fiction. And yet, it is of vital importance for the correct unfolding of the spectacle that this make-believe be scrupulously respected (or else the fiction film is declared "poorly made"), that everything is set to work to make the deception effective and to give it an air of truth (this is the problem of *verisimilitude*).'[25]

This 'problem of verisimilitude' is in fact complicated by the existence of genres, as each genre has its own particular conventions of verisimilitude, over and above those of mainstream narrative fiction as a whole. As Metz implies, verisimilitude is never a question of 'fidelity to the real' (however one defines the real). It is always a function of systems of credibility, of modes of fetishistic belief. Within the overall framework of the 'regime of credibility' that mainstream narrative cinema itself represents, one in which the fetishism of narrative fiction is reduplicated by the fetishism of the cinematic signifier, genres function so as to provide and to institutionalise a variety of the possibilities of fictional credibility allied to a variety of the possibilities of 'cinematic credibility', thus binding the two together all the more strongly as the very ground of cinematic address, as the very basis of the relations between cinema and its spectators.

It should firstly be noted that some genres are conventionally considered to be 'more fictional' than others. Gangster films and war films, for example, tend to be judged according to strict canons of realism, whereas the musical, the gothic horror film and the phantasy/adventure film (i.e. films like *The Thief of Bagdad* or *Jason and the Argonauts*) are recognised as either being more 'poetic' or else as involving more of the faculty of 'imagination', as being closer to 'phantasy' than to 'reality'. This difference stems to a large degree from the status accorded the codes and discourses involved in the two kinds of genre. Those involved in the latter, more immediately 'fictional' genres are always already socially defined as 'fiction' in one way or another. That is to say, these genres consist of bundles of discourses already defined as pertaining to the domain of the subjective, to the domain of imagination and phantasy. At most, they are characterised as representing not factual reality but poetic or psychological realities. As the cinematic signifier is fictional from the outset, a property reinforced by the codes and discourses which combine to construct 'narrative fiction', these social definitions that precede the circulation of any given cinematic genre or text, in their turn reinforce this already double fictionality. Each of these three layers activates and strengthens the fictional potentialities of the others. However, in genres such as war films or gangster films, a number (by no means all) of the discourses and codes deployed overlap with discourses involved in genres socially defined, perhaps not quite as scientific or documentary, but at least as non-fictional, e.g. newspaper reporting, sociology, the adoption of the 'press release' or of the front page headline style characteristic of, for instance, the work of Sam Fuller. In this way, connotations of 'non-fiction' spill over into or become attached to certain genres because some of their component discourses are also produced, classified and circulated by institutions whose business is supposed to be 'facts' and 'truth' rather than fiction and phantasy. This helps to explain why different genres appear to favour different types of source material to legitimise their fiction and anchor their regime of credibility. One type of genres, the less insistently 'fictional' ones, will rely more on pronouncements by state agencies, government documents, history books, biographies, newspapers and newsreels, backed up with blueprints, maps, scale models, etc. On the other hand, the kinds of legitimating documents and references employed in the predominantly 'phantasy' genres will tend to be ancient texts, parapsychological treatises, myths, folklore, religion, etc. In the former, the fiction is balanced across the marks of a socially verified truth, while in the latter it is articulated in terms of socially classified phantasy. The two instances, however, do cross one another in genres like science fiction and psychological horror, where the elements of fiction and phantasy are intermingled with discourses marked as science, i.e. as non-fiction.

Of course, the 'realistic' genres do not involve total belief in the accuracy or the reality of their modes of characterisation, nor in the veracity of their narrative events or diegetic details. The division of belief inherent in all fiction still operates. But the mode of authenticity involved, the regime of credibility inaugurated, produces a balance of belief attenuating or deflecting to some extent the fiction's obvious fictionality, minimising the 'danger' of the spectator being caught in the contradictions lying at the heart of the division itself, the contradictions the 'split' is there to disavow. Of course this 'danger' still remains present and can never be evacuated totally. It can surface whenever there is a clash between the demands of authenticity and those of narrative fiction, which is quite a common occurrence in a genre such as the epic, where the 'reality' of the past that forms the diegetic pretext is so different, so other, so distant, that many of the codes and discourses needed for its construction are either lacking altogether in any verifiable form, or are constantly at odds with the demands of the cinematic institution. The details of costume and decor may be 'right' (though there is always some degree of compromise between 'historical accuracy' and current fashion), but the codes of speech, behaviour and character motivation are often so 'evidently' those of Hollywood rather than those of 'the past' that the balance between the two is easily upset. For example, Howard Hawks makes this point in an interview with Peter Bogdanovich in *Movie*,[26] where, referring to *Land of the Pharaohs*, he complains:

'I don't know how a Pharaoh talks. And Faulkner didn't know. None of us knew . . . It was awfully hard to deepen [the scenes] because we didn't know how those Egyptians thought or what they said . . . You kind of lose all sense of values. You don't know who somebody's for and if you don't have a rooting interest, and you're not for somebody, then you haven't got a picture.'

Generally, though, the balance in these genres is easily managed. The danger is more likely to occur in the genres of 'phantasy', where all the levels involved are heavily invested with marks of the fictional which in turn demands rigorous conventionalisation together with complex signifying strategies if the requirements of credibility are to be fulfilled. It is no accident, therefore, that these genres have persistently been marginalised, relegated to the realms of escapism and utopia (as has the musical) or classified as suitable mainly for children and adolescents. Nor, incidentally, is it any accident that they provide the ground for certain forms of cinephilia, where a fetishistic desire to know 'all about' cinema is concentrated in those forms of cinema in which fetishism is 'most evidently' at work, and in which it is most likely to be 'exposed' as such. The horror film, the phantasy/adventure film and the science fiction film in particular seem to involve special demands on the spectator's faculties of belief and on the cinema's capacities for sustaining it. The degree of 'success' with which this is done is measured by the degree to which particular modes of affect horror, anxiety, fear, wonder—are supposed to be experienced by the spectator. This in itself is indicative of the degree to which these genres are concerned with fetishism and fetishistic modes of belief. Horror, anxiety and fear are all linked to the problematic of castration, while 'wonder' is a function of a division of belief so strong that it often requires the imaginary attribution of two spectators, one of whom is completely duped while the other 'knows better' and is not taken in at all. Alain Bergala, writing about the nature and function of 'children's films', makes the point very clearly:

> 'The term "children's film" in fact functions as a standard of belief, designating a regime of make-believe where the child comes to occupy the imaginary position of the ideally naive, credulous spectator who takes images and fictions at face value. A regime very convenient for parents who in this way give themselves the illusion of accompanying their children to the cinema while it is they, as bashful spectators, who accompany themselves with a false image of childhood as if they dared not occupy the position of the credulous spectator without such delegation.'[27]

Finally, it is worth mentioning here the case of two genres with a special relationship to verisimilitude and to the fetishistic division of belief upon which its various forms depend, even though that relation does not necessarily entail particular consequences for the cinematic signifier itself. The first is that of the detective film, whose system of credibility as a genre depends upon an opposition between the laws of verisimilitude of the world of narrative and the truth that the unfolding of that narrative reveals. Tzvetan Todorov explained this aspect of the detective genre in the following terms:

> 'The revelation, that is, the truth, is incompatible with verisimilitude, as we know from a whole series of detective plots based on the tension between them. In Fritz Lang's film *Beyond a Reasonable Doubt*, this antithesis is taken to extremes. Tom Garrett wants to prove that the death penalty is excessive, that innocent men are often sent to the chair. With the help of his future father-in-law, he selects a crime which is currently baffling the police and pretends to have committed it: he skilfully plants the clues which lead to his own arrest. Up to that point, all the characters in the film believe Garrett to be guilty; but the spectator knows he is innocent—the truth has no verisimilitude, verisimilitude has no truth. Then a double reversal occurs: the police discover documents proving Garrett's innocence, but at the same time we learn that his attitude has been merely a clever way of concealing his crime—it is in fact Garrett who has committed the murder. Again the divorce between truth and verisimilitude is total: if we know Garrett to be guilty, the characters are obliged to believe he is innocent. Only at the end do truth and verisimilitude coincide, but this signifies the death of the character as well as the death of the narrative, which can only continue if there is a gap between truth and verisimilitude.'[28]

The point here is not that verisimilitude is somehow either ignored or foregrounded as investigated, but that the genre has its own laws of verisimilitude, even if this law is, in Todorov's words, the law of anti-verisimilitude:

> 'By relying on anti-verisimilitude, the murder mystery has come under the sway of another verisimilitude, that of its own genre . . . There is something tragic in the fate of the murder mystery writer; his goal is to contest verisimilitude, yet the better he succeeds, the more powerfully he establishes a *new* verisimilitude, one linking his text to the genre to which it belongs.'[29]

What Todorov calls anti-verisimilitude precisely constitutes the basis of this genre's specific regime of verisimilitude. The detective genre turns on this splitting of belief, this fetishistic structure duplicating the fetishistic structure already inherent in cinema itself. As Paul Willemen pointed out in a discussion, the 'red herrings' are the explicit signifiers of this process in operation: they are the signifiers attracting or detouring the look in a process where we know very well they are red herrings, and yet . . . As in *Beyond a Reasonable Doubt*, the 'clues' planted are first red herrings for the readers of the *mise en scène*, i.e. the police, but then are revealed to have been red herrings for the viewers. Fritz Lang's film thus becomes, in Paul Willemen's words, a meditation on red herrings. Similarly, in other detective films, suspects are carefully signalled by means of 'sinister' lighting effects, acting tricks such as voice modulation, suspicious 'looks', 'significant' pauses, or camera movements drawing attention to a suspect presence of an unseen observer, or even close-ups of objects. Anti-verisimilitude only functions in relation to the establishment of a truth, and that truth can only be established if the consistency of the fiction is maintained. The convention of anti-verisimilitude means that 'suspension of disbelief', merely a misleading term for the splitting of belief, is actually integrated into the diegesis as a condition of the inherent narrative structure. It is not only the audience which has to suspend disbelief, it is also the character of the detective, the agent of the process of investigation and representative of the viewer in the diegesis, guiding the reading of the 'events'. But the twist lies, so to speak, in the fact that whereas the fictional detective suspends disbelief in order to discover the truth 'behind' the appearance, the spectator suspends disbelief in order to confirm the illusion, that is to say, the illusion of the fiction itself.

This structure of illusion and belief also constitutes the basis of comedy. Comedy always and above all depends upon an awareness that it is fictional.[30] What comedy does, in its various forms and guises, is to set in motion a narrative process in which various languages, logics, discourses and codes are, at one point or another—at precisely the points of comedy itself—revealed to the audience as fictions. This can occur in two basic forms. Firstly, it can occur in a mode in which the comic text itself periodically stresses its own artifice, in which the comedy stems primarily from the spectator's own credulity. A classic instance of this kind of comedy is Lubitsch's *To Be or Not To Be*, which sets up and constantly shifts between an extraordinarily complex set of layers of artifice and credulity.[31] The opening sequence in particular is exemplary. We are confronted quite clearly by a representation of Adolf Hitler. The figure we see before us is not Hitler himself, but an actor playing Hitler. Equally, however, we are confronted with a desire to suspend our knowledge in order to participate in the construction of a conventional and coherent fiction. After all, there is always a gap between actor and role, especially in instances where the role is that of a real historical figure.[32] There is a clear hesitation here which exists precisely because the gap is not fully closed, as it were, by the address of the text at this point: the parodic commentary prevents that. Similarly, when we move on to what appears initially to be a scene taking place in the headquarters of a Nazi general, there is a hesitation initiated by the fact that there is no textual indication that the scene is not to be read 'straight'—i.e. that it is not to be taken at 'face value'—while on the other hand, the general is played by Jack Benny, the star of the film and known comic actor. It is only when we are shown that the scene we have been witnessing is a theatrical rehearsal that we know definitively that it is not 'real' in fictional, diegetic terms. But then, of course, our belief, our credulity, has only shifted one step back, so to speak, to the level of the meta-scene within which the rehearsal scene has taken place.

The alternative mode of comedy is one that only plays on the languages, the logics, discourses and codes which the text highlights within the diegesis and the fictional characters' relationships to them. This mode of comedy plays on verbal 'wit', confronting or overlaying one discursive logic with another as in Marx Brothers comedies; or plays on disjunctions between discourses, modes of dress, behaviour etc. in different classes or social groups as in the comedy of Frank Capra. In this type of comedy, the spectator is maintained in a continuous and undisturbed mode of belief, against which the modes of belief of the characters in the discourses they inhabit/employ are measured. Although it remains the case that the nature of the spectator's credulity, unquestioned as it may be, is such that a recognition of the fiction as fiction remains far more essential than in other fictional modes.

In both modes, at both ends of the spectrum of comedy, the comic effect itself derives from a triple structure of belief, with credulity, 'knowledge', and fetishism proper as the three constant functions which are disturbed variously across the two basic instances of subjectivity involved: that of the characters in the fiction, and that of the spectators of the fiction.

*   *   *

Scopophilia and fetishism do not exist separately in mainstream cinema. They are interrelated in particular and determinate ways, firstly, across the instance of the image itself: lack 'filled' by detail as in Ophuls' images, by *mise en scene* and colour as in Nicholas Ray's work, by composition as in Murnau, by framing as in Welles' cinema—the subject held in the plenitude of the organisation of the image; and secondly, through the organisation as narrative, where lack is 'filled' through linear narrative flow, scopophilia engaged and contained in the movement from image to image, articulated as the visual mastery—the distance—of a coherence of point of view.

Fetishism and scopophilia are also each implicated in the various moments of knowledge and belief that mainstream cinema entails, especially in so far as they are articulated with yet another of the drives that cinema engages: epistemophilia, the desire to know, to 'find out'. Clearly this drive is also a central component both of narrative itself and, especially, of the hermeneutic code isolated by Roland Barthes in his analysis of Balzac's short story *Sarrasine*.[33] The hermeneutic code moves the reader through the text by evoking questions and postponing answers up to the final conclusion.

All genres operate a conjunction of these drives and structures, and although they cannot, in my opinion, be consistently distinguished the one from the other in terms of particular balances between them, nevertheless, a number of genres do involve quite specific structural combinations of some or of all of them. In this way they can be said to fulfil what I have argued to be their primary function: that is to say, they function as instances of variation and regulation determining regimes of controlled variety.

The detective film, for example, and certain versions of the thriller, are marked by a particularly overt and insistent hermeneutic structure: the restoration of narrative equilibrium is conditional upon the establishment of a knowledge as to the cause or causes of the event initiating the narrative in the first place—a murder, a disappearance, a theft, a threat of blackmail, or whatever. The process of the narrative is a process of investigation, both on the part of the fictional detective or of the character who performs an analogous role, and on the part of the spectator. Like the detective, the spectator is constantly looking for clues and signs in a process of piecing together the reasons for the process of the crime, attempting to solve the enigma which structures the story. Hence the detective film and the thriller are genres which, so to speak, actively acknowledge and inscribe within their structures the practice of reading. Of course, they do so only in a containing and limited way, by means of an enclosed and linear hermeneutic structure, which is, precisely, a characteristic and defining convention of the genre itself.

Both the detective genre and the thriller inscribe the spectating subject as caught up in a particular version of epistemophilia, always engaging it to be 'satisfied', to be given the answer to the riddle. In other words, always engaging it in terms of the structure of fetishism. This is not by accident: disavowal and the desire to know are in fact always co-extensive, with epistemophilia being constantly displaced in order to preserve the fissure supporting/necessitating the fetish. Indeed it might be argued that fetishism itself is the product of the articulation of both these instances together, that it is a structure founded upon the modalities of the epistemophilic drive: the desire to know *and* disavowal, together, articulate a desire to know something else, a substitute for what in fact is at stake. The process of finding out is thus represented in relation to that which one wishes to avoid knowing. What is specific to the detective film and the thriller is the fact that this co-extensiveness is persistently demonstrated though never exposed to the fissure supporting it. It is not a matter of identifying or of finding the 'fetish' incarnated in any given clue, or in the last piece that makes the jigsaw 'fit', restoring a complete picture. On the contrary, it is the

42

jigsaw puzzle itself, the story of the crime that represents the structure of fetishism, the process of its institution and elaboration binding the spectator into the structure of (split) belief. In the detective and thriller genres, this story functions to restore 'law and order' in an overt and literal way: what 'fills the gap', what sutures the wound that the crime both represents and opens up, is, precisely, a narrative scarred by red herrings.

In the cinema as a whole, the epistemophilic component of fetishism is predominantly though by no means exclusively articulated via the scopic drive. It is then not surprising that the inscription of epistemophilia across the hermeneutic structures of the detective film and the thriller should constantly and characteristically involve quite overt diegetic references to voyeurism. Think, for example, of Polanski's *Chinatown* and of Altman's *The Long Goodbye*, films which construct a whole set of discourses about voyeurism around the character of the private eye. Or think of individual scenes in any number of detective films and thrillers in which the central protagonist is engaged, simply, in secretive looking. It is worth noting in this context that the many celebrated instances of voyeurism, exhibitionism and fetishism in the films of Alfred Hitchcock[34] are, partly at least, a function of the fact that Hitchcock makes thrillers: the thriller is a genre that consists of the elaboration of a narrative under the sign of these three drives, they are part—and arguably the dominant part—of the conditions of existence of the genre. It is also worth pointing out the extent to which the detective film and the thriller inscribe all these elements into the very fabric of the film text itself through the deployment of a heavy and insistent chiaroscuro giving rise to the sub-genre known as *film noir*. Darkness not only signifies concealment, invoking an unknown and unseen presence within it (thereby simultaneously invoking the desire to know and the desire to see); it is also a figure of absence and lack. Darkness is the edge between presence (that which it conceals) and absence (that which it is), and its ambiguity in this respect is reflected in its status *vis-à-vis* the cinematic signifier on the one hand and the diegesis of the other. It is not fully, completely and unambiguously a property of the narrative world, yet neither is it simply a property of the cinematic signifier as such. It hovers, oscillates between the two, thereby inscribing scopophilia and epistemophilia in relation to both.[35]

There is also, of course, a strong chiaroscuro tradition in the horror film, with shadow playing a similar role in relation both to epistemophilia and to the scopic drive. They frequently figure together, for instance, in those moments of suspense that centre on the appearance of a monster. Such moments are marked by a fascination with the monstrous that extends across the whole process of the narrative, and that exists despite, or rather all the more strongly because of, the elements of fear and anxiety that are simultaneously and inseparately involved. The precise nature of that fascination becomes clearer once it is recognised that all the elements involved here are central to the problematic of castration and that the horror film—centrally concerned with the fact and the effects of difference—invariably involves itself in that problematic and invariably mobilises specific castration anxieties. It does so, however, not so as radically to undermine the spectating subject, to expose the drives it

43

mobilises in the lack upon which they are founded, but to entertain it, to produce it in the coherence of a process, as a filling in, something which, given the specific articulation of the problematic of castration, involves an equally specific set of interrelated instances of fetishism. Hence the monster may represent the lack, but precisely by doing so it in fact functions to fill the lack with its own presence, thus coming to function as a fetish, simultaneously representing and disavowing the problems of sexual difference at stake. A process illustrated by the fact that many cinematic monsters have become favourite fetish images, as is evident from the enormous number of picture books, masks and toys devoted to them. A number of different strategies are used to stage the monster's appearance(s). Generally speaking, these appearances oscillate throughout the narrative, setting up a rhythm of presence and absence, with the movement of the film's narrative geared towards finding the appropriate means to symbolise and regulate that process through the appropriate formula or object, and thus to contain that irrevocable lack in the place of which the monster emerges. In this respect the play with the monster's appearance/disappearance is analogous to the *fort/da* game, the game of repeatedly making something appear and disappear. In *The Four Fundamental Concepts of Psychoanalysis,* Jacques Lacan stresses that the *fort* (gone) and the *da* (here) are not simple instances of presence on the one hand and absence on the other, with repetition constituting an oscillation between the two. On the contrary, both moments, as signifiers, are constructed in relation to absence, and therefore the game as a whole functions in relation to a fundamental and irrevocable lack that it serves only to contain (not to master) through the process of its repetition as a structure:

> 'The activity as a whole symbolises repetition, but not at all that of some need that might demand the return of the mother and which would be expressed in a simple cry. It is the repetition of the mother's departure as cause of a *Spaltung* (split) in the subject—overcome by the alternating game, *fort-da*, which is a *here or there,* and whose aim, in its alternation, is simply that of being the *fort* of a *da,* and the *da* of a *fort*. It is aimed at what, essentially, is not there, *qua* represented—for it is the game itself that is the *Representanz* of the *Vorstellung*.'[36]

But whatever strategy is used to stage the monster's mode of presence, it is a rule in mainstream cinema that whenever any kind of monster is involved, it must appear visibly at some point: a rule responsible for the problems Tourneur had with *Night of the Demon* (*Curse of the Demon*). This insistence is less a matter of commercial insensitivity to the subtleties of an artist, but more a fact deriving from the special way the problematic of castration underpins the horror film. Where monsters of the kind being discussed here do not figure at all, the 'horror' and its sources and effects tend to be addressed more 'directly'. In *Psycho,* for example, the interrelationship between castration and the constitution of sexual identity is clearly articulated, while Corman's Poe films constitute a veritable anthology of the ways in which the eye can come to figure in castration fantasies.[37]

Interconnected with this function of the monster is the enormous stress laid not only on the moment(s) of its appearance, but also on the nature of its appearance. All the resources of the costume and make-up department are mobilised precisely to give the monster an appearance and an appearance that will not only frighten and terrify, but will also give it credence, an instance of the operation of the 'splitting of belief' fundamental to the structure of fetishism, and one which is merely part of a whole battery of such instances in the horror film, in which are invested all the faculties of cinematic 'trucage' (tricks, special effects and so on) that the cinematic institution can afford.[38] Moreover, it is no accident that the most 'spectacular' and intricate—the most arresting—mobilisation of 'trucage' centres so frequently either on the initial appearance of the monster or on its ultimate destruction; or even more tellingly, on its birth, the process of its construction 'there before our very eyes', an essential ingredient of the Frankenstein films, of the Jekyll and Hyde versions, the werewolf films and Hammer's *Dracula* series. A corollary of its birth is its disintegration—again, before our very eyes— as for instance in the first Hammer *Dracula*. These moments are significant and symptomatic because they are the pivotal moments in the fascination that the horror film involves, marking the 'turn' of the fetishistic division of belief upon which it is based.

The horror film, then, is a veritable festival of fetishistic effects, a complex imbrication of a whole variety of fetishistic structures and mechanisms operating across a number of distinct levels, each acting to reinforce the others. It is scarcely surprising, therefore, that the horror film is concerned so centrally not only with curiosity, knowledge and belief, but also, and crucially, with their transgressive and 'forbidden' forms and with the establishment of the terms and consequences in relation to which such forms are to be understood. It is thus also scarcely surprising that the discourses of the horror film are so frequently saturated with religion, while the critical discourses accompanying the genre are rooted in mysticism and other forms of irrationalism.

Notes

[1] C. Metz, 'The Imaginary Signifier', in *Screen*, Vol 16, no 2, p. 18.

[2] P. Willemen, 'Tashlin's Method: An Hypothesis', in C. Johnston and P. Willemen (eds), *Frank Tashlin*, Edinburgh Film Festival, 1973, pp. 122–124.

[3] Stephen Heath, 'Film and System: Terms of Analysis–Pt 1', in *Screen*, Vol 16, no 2, 1975, p. 99.

[4] P. Willemen, 'Notes on Subjectivity' in *Screen*, Vol 19, no 1, Spring 1978, pp. 58–59: 'Each text is in fact a network of intersecting and overlapping statements: quotations, references, derivations, inversions, etc. A text, any text, consists of a bundle of discourses, each discourse installing its subject of enunciation. This also means that it is misleading to describe a text as a signifying chain, i.e. *one* discursive operation corresponding to one subject-production. As texts are imbrications of discourses, they must necessarily produce series of subject positions. But these subjects can be (and are) mapped on to each other, pulled into place.'

[5] S. Heath, 'Film Performance' in *Cinetracts,* Vol 1, no 2, 1977, p. 9.

[6] T. Todorov, 'Detective Fiction' in *The Poetics of Prose*, Cornell University Press, 1977, pp. 44–47: 'At the base of the whodunit we find a duality, and it is this duality which will guide our description. This novel contains not one but two stories: the story of the crime and the story of the investigation. We might further characterise these two stories by saying that the first–the story of the crime–tells "what really happened", whereas the second–the story of the investigation–explains "how the reader (or the narrator) has come to know about it". The fundamental point is that this duality is articulated as a duality of times, of temporal orders.'

[7] R. Barthes, 'Structural Analysis of Narratives' in *Image, Music, Text,* S. Heath (ed), London 1978, p. 119.

[8] Ibid.

[9] P. Mellencamp, 'Spectacle and Spectator: Looking Through the American Musical Comedy' in *Cinetracts*, Vol 1, no 2, 1977.

[10] Ibid.

[11] S. Heath, 'Narrative Space' in *Screen*, Vol 17, no 3, 1976, p. 90.

[12] Ibid, p. 97.

[13] Ibid.

[14] C. Metz, op. cit., p. 42.

[15] Op. cit., p. 47.

[16] Op. cit., p. 48.

[17] Op. cit., p. 62.

[18] See S. Heath, 'Narrative Space', op. cit., and 'Anata Mo' in *Screen*, Vol 17, no 4; P. Willemen, 'Voyeurism, The Look and Dwoskin' in *Afterimage*, no 6.

[19] C. Metz, op. cit., p. 62.

[20] Op. cit., p. 64.

[21] Op. cit., p. 63.

[22] C. Metz, 'Histoire/Discourse, Notes on Two Voyeurisms' in *Edinburgh '76 Magazine*, no 1, p. 24.

[23] Laura Mulvey, 'Visual Pleasure and Narrative Cinema' in *Screen*, Vol 6, no 3, and 'You don't know what is happening, do you Mr. Jones' in *Spare Rib*, no 8; D. Dubroux's review of *Fedora* in *Cahiers du Cinéma*, no 294 (English translation in *Fedora*, programme note available from BFI/EAS).

[24] C. Metz, 'The Imaginary Signifier', op. cit., p. 66.

[25] Op. cit., p. 70.

[26] *Movie*, no 5, 1962, p. 17.

[27] 'Dora and the Magic Lantern' in *Cahiers du Cinéma*, no 287.

[28] T. Todorov, *The Poetics of Prose*, Cornell Univ. Press, 1977, pp. 85–86.

[29] Ibid., pp. 86–87.

[30] Octave Mannoni, 'L'Illusion Comique ou le Théâtre du point de vue de l'Imaginaire' in *Clefs pour l'Imaginaire*, Le Seuil, Paris, 1969, esp. pp. 164–169.

[31] For a detailed discussion of *To Be or Not To Be* in terms of shifts in layers of artifice and conventions, see Sheila Whitaker's analysis in *Framework*, no 5, 1976/77.

[32] See Jean Louis Comolli's essay 'Historical Fiction—A Body Too Much' in *Screen*, Vol 19, no 2, 1978.

[33] R. Barthes, *S/Z*, Jonathan Cape Ltd, London 1975.

[34] Peter Wollen, 'Hitchcock's Vision' in *Cinema*, no 3.

[35] For a discussion of the role of chiaroscuro in the thriller, highlighting some of the points at issue here, see Paul Willemen's 'Notes Towards the Construction of Readings of Tourneur' in *Jacques Tourneur*, edited by Paul Willemen and Claire Johnston, Edinburgh Film Festival, 1975, esp. pp. 23–26.

[36] J. Lacan, *The Four Fundamental Concepts of Psychoanalysis*, Hogarth Press, 1977, pp. 61–63.

[37] See for instance Karl Abraham's essay on scopophilia in his *Selected Papers*, Hogarth Press, 1978.

[38] For a discussion of 'trucage' and of the instances of fetishistic belief that those forms entail, see Christian Metz, 'Trucage et Cinéma' in *Essais sur la signification au cinéma*, Vol 11, Paris 1972. A (poor) translation of this essay appeared in *Critical Enquiry*, Vol 2, no 4, 1977.

Chapter 3

In the preceding chapters it has been argued that genres constitute specific variations of the interplay of codes, discursive structures and drives involved in the whole of mainstream cinema. On the other hand, the point was made that genres cannot, in fact, be systematically characterised and differentiated one from another solely on the basis of such instances, taken in isolation as if they constituted specific generic essences. Time and time again it emerged that generic specificity is extremely difficult to pin down in general statements that are anything other than rudimentary and banal, such as: the narrative setting of the western is that of the American frontier; the gangster film involves the depiction of organised crime in the context of industrial capitalism; the melodrama centres its narrative structure on the vicissitudes of heterosexual love, etc. The apparent contradiction here is an important one, since it is symptomatic of the very nature of the genres themselves as systemic processes and, also, it is indicative of their function to produce regularised variety. The appearance of the contradiction is due, in other words, to the fact that genres are instances of repetition and difference.

Repetition and difference have firstly to be understood in their relationship to desire, pleasure and *jouissance*, i.e. as modalities of the process of the subject. Desire is always a function of both repetition and difference. It is founded in the difference between on the one hand the initial experience of pleasure, the mark established by that experience and which functions as its signifier(s), and on the other, future attempts to repeat the experience, future repetitions of the signifier(s). Desire is hence also founded on the urge to repeat and the impossibility of ever being able to do so. The reproduction of the signifier allows satisfaction, but it is a satisfaction marked by the gap between signifier and experience. The existence of the gap is the reason for the inexhaustibility of desire, but it also allows whatever satisfaction is attainable to be renewed. Hence pleasure lies both in the repetition of the signifier(s) and in the limited but nonetheless fundamental difference underpinning and separating such instances of repetition. The subject is maintained in an oscillation that thus rarely threatens either its pleasure or its existence. That threat only occurs in moments of *jouissance*: the possibility of 'total' pleasure, the extinction of desire, of death. Or, as Paul Willemen explains:

> 'The term *jouissance* is an untranslatable term used by some psychoanalysts to suggest a "beyond pleasure", intimately linking desire and death with the death drive as the dominant partner. Pleasure is located in the moment of homeostasis between tension and its release, in the zero between before and after. But whereas pleasure is founded on the (quasi) repeatability of such moments, i.e. the possibility to annul the moment of annulation of tension, *jouissance* relates to the freezing of such a zero, to the representation of annulation which is not reversible (i.e. death).'[1]

Hence Roland Barthes' distinction:

'Text of pleasure: the text that contents, fills, grants euphoria; the text that comes from culture and does not break with it, is linked to a *comfortable* practice of reading. Text of bliss (jouissance): the text that imposes a state of loss, the text that discomforts (perhaps to the point of boredom), unsettles the reader's historical, cultural, psychological assumptions, the consistency of his tastes, values, memories, brings to a crisis his relation with language.'[2]

The mainstream narrative is nothing if not a 'text of pleasure': a text that regulates the subject's desire for pleasure, that functions, therefore, according to a precise economy of difference (the movement of desire, the subject ceaselessly in process) and of repetition (the containment of that movement, its repletion, the subject ceaselessly closed through the recuperation of difference in figures of tightly bound symmetry). Stephen Heath offered the following formulation for this process:

'The coherence of any text depends on a sustained equilibrium of new informations, points of advance, and anaphoric recalls, ties that make fast, hold together. One part of the particularity of classic cinema is its exploitation of narrative in the interests of an extreme tendency towards coalescence, an economic tightness of totalization; the film is gathered up on a whole series of rimes in which elements—of both "form" and "content"—are found, shifted and turned back symmetrically, as in a mirror.'[3]

The spectator, then, is maintained as subject in an economy of narration through the articulation of desire. The mainstream narrative text operates as a binding of desire in the figuration of coherence, a coherence that is specified anew in each individual text through its own particular textual system (each film consists of its difference from any other). This system engages specific versions of the figures, functions and logics allowed by the economy of the mainstream system (in this respect, each film is an instance of repetition of this system itself, the same as any other mainstream film).

Genres intervene between the two instances of process, of subject regulation: that of the mainstream narrative and that of the individual text. Genres thus establish a regulation of the variety of mainstream narrative across a series of individual texts, organising and systematising the difference that each text represents, filling in the gap between text and system. For example, genres can be directly related to the textual economy of the mainstream narrative in that they systematise its regime of difference and repetition, specifying its rhythm of oscillation between the two. In this way genres function to move the subject from text to text and from text to narrative system, binding these instances together into a constant coherence, the coherence of the cinematic institution. In doing so, genres themselves are marked by a similar economy of repetition and difference. If the nature of that economy can perhaps best be characterised as one of repetition and limited difference, it should, however, be stressed that the element of difference is not only real but fundamental. The notion that 'all westerns (or all gangster films, or all war films, or whatever) are the same' is not just an unwarranted generalisation, it is profoundly wrong: if each text within a genre were, literally, the same, there would simply not be enough difference to generate either meaning or pleasure. Hence there would be no audience. Difference is absolutely essential to the economy of genre. As Jacques Lacan stressed, 'Repetition demands the new'. Moreover, repetition and difference are themselves not separable, either as 'entities', so to speak, or, even, as tendencies: they function as a relation. There is hence not repetition *and* difference, but repetition *in* difference. Bearing in mind the nature of the economy of genre, an economy of variation rather than of rupture, a better formulation as far as genre is concerned would be: difference *in* repetition.

The mechanism which produces this element of difference in each instance of repetition at the level of the individual text has been outlined by Yuri Lotman as follows:

> 'Repetition means the same as equivalence, which emerges as the basis of an incomplete sameness, where there is one level (or more) at which the elements are the same together with one (or more) at which they aren't. Equivalence cannot be reduced to a dead uniformity; which is precisely why it includes dissimilarity. Similar levels organise dissimilar ones in that they establish relations of similarity within them, while simultaneously dissimilar levels work in the opposite direction, pointing up difference within similarity.'[4]

The same kind of mechanism is at work on the level of genre itself, where it is similarly the case that what is involved is not simply a single system but rather a combination of several systems, so that any instance of repetition is always subject to the modifications that that combination produces. For instance, this proposition has a number of consequences for the notions of iconography. Visual signifiers are usually held to constitute 'icons' (i.e. signifiers of a particular genre) if they are subject to regular occurrences, i.e. repetitions. Their function is generally considered to be the establishment of a stable framework of signs in relation to which difference and variation can be both produced on the one hand and read and understood on the other. However, once it is established that repetition always involves an element of difference, that difference and variation are properties not only of the elements outside the framework so to speak, but also of the framework itself, then the nature and function of iconography have to be re-thought, if, indeed, the term is to be retained at all. Iconography would consist not of individual visual signifiers, repeated identically across a series of generic texts, nor even of the relations between them, conceived as the function of a single system, but rather of the 'rules' governing both the successive appearances of those signifiers and the transformations to which they are subject. Its function would consist in the provision of that which systematises both repetition and difference at the level of the visual image.

At the root of the presence of difference in repetition, and at the root of the mechanisms which govern its manifestation, is the fact of the existence of process. It is this, above all, that is responsible not only for the double-edged nature of iconography, but for the double-edged nature of genres themselves, one in which a rule-bound element and an element of transgression are both equally important. It is process, therefore, that accounts for the contradiction outlined at the beginning of this chapter. It accounts, on the one hand, for the fact that genres appear to constitute clearly defined systems and, on the other, for the fact that they are rarely, if ever, susceptible to detailed analysis as such. As Jean-Louis Leutrat noted in his analysis of the western genre:

'Genre being the locus par excellence of repetition and difference, it is necessary to disengage both the constant and the variable elements. This operation requires a prior diachronic investigation, as variation manifests itself in the course of a historical development. By the same token, it is impossible to give a definition of a genre. All one can do is remain on the level of observation and note some facts. One can confirm the existence of the genre when one has disengaged a series of "works related to each other by means of a structure that establishes a continuity and which is manifested in a historical series".'[5]

Genres, then, are not systems: they are processes of systematisation. It is only as such that they can perform the role allotted them by the cinematic institution. It is only as such that they can function to provide, simultaneously, both regulation and variety.

*　　　　*　　　　*

The stress throughout this booklet has been on the discursive aspects of any genre, on the way in which individual genres systematise the different functions and effects of mainstream cinema. This has meant that two aspects of genre, in particular, have not been discussed directly. On the one hand there is the economic aspect. Genres, of course, do exist within the context of a set of economic relations and practices, a fact often stressed by pointing out that they are the forms of the products of capitalist industry. On the other hand there is the fact that genres exist not simply as a body of texts, or a body of textual conventions, but also as a set of expectations. To quote Jean-Louis Leutrat again:

'The only way a genre model or genre rules can be said to exist is as . . . a memorial metatext and on that level alone. It is because viewers/readers operate with sets of expectations and levels of predictability that it is possible to perceive instances of variation, repetition, rectification and modification. In this way, genre can be considered as one single continuous text.'[6]

These two aspects are extremely important, and so I intend to discuss them as a conclusion to my overall argument. But rather than treat them separately, I want to take them together, particularly in so far as they intersect with one another at the point of exhibition/consumption. Here the interrelation between them can be clearly seen as a function of the fact that films or rather viewings of films are commodities of a specific kind. However, as a preamble, it is necessary to say a few words about the economic dimension of genre as it exists at the point of production.

Genres are not the product of economic factors as such. The conditions provided by the capitalist economy account neither for the existence of the particular genres that have hitherto been produced, nor for the existence of the conventions that constitute them. However, genre itself, as a framework for production, and as a form of organisation of the product, clearly has a relationship to such factors and is clearly, in part at least, determined by them. The effects of that relationship can be traced especially in the functioning of genre *vis-à-vis* the exigencies of the necessity for profit, on the one hand, and *vis-à-vis* the contradictions engendered at the level of production by the fact that films are artistic commodities (commodities of a particular and peculiar kind) on the other.

The often used argument that there is a built-in tendency towards genre in the very pressures for profitability that governs the operation of the mainstream film industry, while true in a general sense, can be misleading if taken solely at the level of individual genre films. That is to say, if taken to refer to a mechanism by which genres are created simply by repeating the formulae marking those individual films which happen to have been financially successful. Within the period of the studio system, certainly, profit was calculated not in relation to individual films, but rather in relation to series of films, those produced within a particular time-span or within a particular cycle of production. When linked to the fact of economic pressures towards the maximisation of capital assets, and to the concomitant forms of production organisation these pressures give rise to, the economic importance of genre becomes evident: genres serve as basic and 'convenient' units for the calculation of investment and profit, and as basic and 'convenient' categories in which to organise capital assets so as to ensure that their capacity will be utilised to the maximum. Economic factors can therefore be seen to exert a pressure which results not perhaps in the creation of genres as such, but rather in their perpetuation as the basic form that the industry's products take. If they do not account for the existence of specific genres, they do account for the ways in which individual films tend constantly to be planned and constructed in generic terms, for the ways in which individual films tend constantly either to be produced as, or to become, genre films.

From the point of view of film production, one particular aspect of the nature of the commodities produced is especially important: in contrast to other, non-artistic commodities, each film, of whatever variety, kind or genre has in some way to be different, unique in order to guarantee regimes of pleasure and meaning, as outlined earlier. The implications of this can best be illustrated by comparing the way in which diversity and difference function in industries making non-artistic products, with the ways in which they function in the film industry.

The motor car industry, to take a random example of the former, does not restrict itself to the manufacture of only one model of car. This is due not only to the fact that it comprises a number of different enterprises, each in competition with the others, and each, therefore, offering a variety of models in order to gain a bigger share of the market. It is also due to the fact that, in any event, the industry as a whole has constantly to stimulate demand. Comparing models to genres, a fundamental difference in function becomes apparent, a difference related to the nature of the commodities concerned. Whereas each individual car made according to the specifications of any one model should, ideally, be identical to all the others, each individual film belonging to a particular genre has to be different. Whereas, in other words, models in the car industry function to produce diversity, genres in the film industry function primarily to contain it. Genres, therefore, are crucial to the film industry. They provide, simultaneously, maximum regularity and economy in the utilisation of plant and personnel, and the minimum degree of difference necessary for each individual product.

It is at this point that I would like to discuss the point of interaction between economics and the nature of genre as a set of expectations. One peculiarity of the commodities produced by the film industry has been noted above: each product has to be different from all the others. There are two others that need to be taken into account. The first is that what the consumer buys at the box office is not a film as such, but the right to view a film. The second is that this right gives access to a process, rather than to a product in the conventional empirical sense. The residue of this process is memory, and it is this which the consumer, so to speak, takes home. John Ellis has outlined these characteristics as follows:

'It is commonplace that the cinema is an institution that has an economic and an ideological face. It is usually deduced from this fact that the cinema has to make a profit, and that it makes ideas that lull the masses pleasurably. Contrary to this multiplication of the possible products of cinema, I would venture to suggest that cinema does not really produce anything. This, like most things, is not as extraordinary as it first sounds. To say that the cinema produces films is plainly inadequate: films as strips of celluloid in cans are without great value, certainly not meriting the amounts expended on their production. The formula "cinema produces films" refuses to ask the question of what a film is. The Palache Report on the British cinema in 1944 is more enlightening: "A cinematographic film represents something more than a mere commodity to be bartered against others" . . . Films, then, are themselves processes rather than products: capital is turned over by the industry through people paying to see a film, not to buy a copy of it (i.e. paying for the *possibility* of pleasure). These processes that are films turn upon the perpetual production of representations that are addressed to a viewing subject; they effect a perpetual placing of the subject in relation to desire— a continual process that we are pleased to call pleasurable. To begin to talk about the product of the cinema is very problematic. Cinema does not *produce* the subject through the film in the sense that the family does; perhaps the only products of the process of film are marginal ones, the memory of a film (important nonetheless to all kinds of activities: fantasies, enlightenment about psychology, a knowledge of the world etc.) and the image of a film (its insertion into other practices of representation, e.g. a review).'[7]

The problem for the industry, stemming from these characteristics, is that it needs, as far as possible, to guarantee meaning and pleasure (pleasurable forms of meaning) in order to attract and to maintain an audience sizeable enough to produce a return on its capital. If it is in any way to do this, it has to institution-alise a set of expectations which it will be able, within the limits of its economic and ideological practices, to fulfil. These expectations exist on a number of levels. There is the expectation, for example, as to what a film itself is, and as to what overall pleasures it will afford. These are almost always met, since they exist as a function of the very basis of mainstream cinema in narrative and spectacle. There are other, more specific expectations, those to do with the star system and with genre especially, but also those to do, for example, with author-ship. In many ways authorship can be considered as functioning analogously to genre: both provide limited (contained and coherent) variety, both engage similar economies of repetition and difference, and both regulate the display of cinema, its potential excess, whether on the one hand as a generic system or, on the other, as personal style. The points of their intersection merely multiply the instances of cinematic variety while simultaneously controlling and contain-ing them, limiting the danger in difference.

As far as genre is concerned, expectations exist both to be satisfied, and, also, to be redefined. There is thus, so to speak, a double layer of expectation. One level concerns the meeting of a set of basic conventional requirements. The other concerns the necessity for novelty and difference. Hence John Ellis' remarks:

'Just as it is inevitable that any film will be impelled into some kind of category and some kind of context, it is also inevitable that most films will go beyond the image that such contexts and categories produce. It is this tension that makes the history of cinema: the tension between commodity (the offering of pleasure in context, the narrative-image of a film) and process (the placing and displacing of the narrative economy, the movement towards memory and the balance of novelty and repetition).'[8]

These expectations are based, certainly, on the memories produced in view-ing—hence the phrase 'memorial metatext'. Indeed one of the main functions of genre is the containment and regulation of cinematic memory: its instances of repetition, in particular, serve constantly as points of cinematic recall. But they are also, and importantly, based on, produced and circulated by all those institu-tionalised practices that together function to produce what Ellis refers to as the 'image' of films: reviewing, criticism, advertising, and so on. Viewing, memory and image together produce that homogeneity of expectation appropriate not simply to genre itself, but also to the industry as a whole, and, hence, to the economic imperatives it is subject to.

It is thus at this point that the two levels, the two aspects of genre can be brought together. Any one genre is, simultaneously, a coherent and systematic body of film texts, and a coherent and systematic set of expectations. As well as providing a means of regulating desire across a series of textual instances, and of offering an ordered variety of the discursive possibilities of cinema itself, genres also provide a means of regulating memory and expectation, a means of containing the possibilities of reading. Overall, they offer the industry a means of controlling demand, and the institution a means of containing coherently the effects that its products produce.

Notes

[1] Paul Willemen, 'Notes Towards the Construction of Readings of Tourneur' in *Jacques Tourneur*, P. Willemen and C. Johnston (eds), Edinburgh 1975, p. 35.
[2] Roland Barthes, *The Pleasure of the Text*, London 1976, p. 14.
[3] Stephen Heath, 'The Question Oshima' in *Wide Angle*, Vol 12, no 1, 1977, p. 55.
[4] Yuri Lotman, *La Structure du Texte Artistique*, Paris 1973, p. 131.
[5] Jean-Louis Leutrat, *Le Western*, Paris 1973, p. 22. The final sentence is a quote from Hans-Robert Jauss' article in *Poétique*, no 1, p. 82.
[6] Jean-Louis Leutrat, op. cit., pp. 35–6.
[7] John Ellis, 'The Institution of Cinema' in *Edinburgh '77 Magazine*, C. Johnston (ed), Edinburgh 1977, p. 37.
[8] John Ellis, 'Writing, filming and context: A reply to Mark Nash' in *Screen Education*, no 27, pp. 94–5.

Appendix A: Genre and Sexuality

Under the pressure of feminism and of the women's movement in particular, sexuality and the production/inscription of 'images' of men and women have been important issues in the analysis of the cinema. Cinema has almost from the outset been recognised as having an important social role to play in the construction and provision of images and definitions of masculinity and femininity but it is only recently that some of the mechanisms and processes involved have begun to be adequately examined. What I want to do here is to introduce this issue into the discussion of genre and to say something about a number of individual genres in the light of theoretical ideas that have been developed in recent years.

As versions of mainstream cinema, offering systematised variants on its modes of meaning and pleasure, genres participate constantly in an ongoing process of construction of sexual difference and sexual identity. This is not simply a consequence of the fact that some genres (like the western and the war film) have traditionally been defined as aiming at a 'male' audience, while others (like the melodrama and the musical) have traditionally been defined as aiming at a 'female' one. While it is true that the cinematic institution has itself tended to categorise certain of its genres and certain of its individual films in this way, and while it has often evaluated the market for its products in such terms, it is nevertheless the case that it has always, also, sought to cater for *both* sexes, whatever the intended audience might be. In this way, of course, it has contributed doubly to the construction and the maintenance of sexual identity and difference—by constructing, labelling and marketing films and genres according to (equally constructed) categories of gender and by simultaneously inscribing them with 'points of appeal' which it marks and defines as specific either to one sex or the other. It is also a question of the fact that sexual identity and sexual difference are inscribed inevitably into a system of signification (especially one designed to narrate the actions and activities of human characters), and into the subject relations that that system, and its various processes, sustains.

Quite evidently, there are a number of different aspects of this issue, each equally important and each equally complex.[1] All I want to do here, finally, is to pose some questions and outline some ideas in relation to one such aspect: the way in which sexual identity and sexual difference are focused in their construction on the representation of the human body, and the way in which such representations are specified generically. One of the dimensions to this particular aspect of the problem, that of the articulation of the body and the look, and of the relations of the subject in that articulation, has, rightly, been the subject of much discussion. This discussion has concentrated in particular on the extent to which it is the body of the woman which is featured as the point of spectacle, which is privileged as the object of the look. Paul Willemen takes up precisely this point from Laura Mulvey's seminal article *Visual Pleasure and the Narrative Cinema*. He argues that both the female and the male body can be situated as spectacle in the scopic drive. While recognising that, nevertheless, under patriarchy, it is the former in particular that is subject to the apparatus of specularisation, Willemen argues that:

'It is true that traditional forms of cinema are dedicated to the legitimisation and perpetuation of a patriarchal order, and that in such a context, the object of the look is traditionally the female form displayed for the gaze and enjoyment of men as active controllers of the look. However, the real basis for the distinction between direct scopophilic contact with the object of desire and mediated contact/possession of that object must be sought in the origins of the scopophilic drive itself. In *Instincts and Their Vicissitudes* Freud wrote that "At the beginning of its activity, the scopophilic instinct is auto-erotic: it has indeed an object, but that object is the subject's own body".

The identification of the woman as the privileged object of the scopophilic drive is therefore already the product of a displacement. Mulvey doesn't allow sufficient room for the fact that in patriarchy the direct object of the scopophilic desire can also be male. If scopophilic pleasure relates primarily to the observation of one's sexual like (as Freud suggests), then the two looks distinguished by Mulvey (i.e. the look at the object of desire and the look at one's sexual like) are in fact varieties of one single mechanism: the repression of homosexuality. The narcissistic identification with the ideal ego in the diegesis would therefore not be a mere mediation in order to get at a desired woman, but the contemplation of the male hero would in itself be a substantial source of gratification for a male viewer—as is demonstrated time and time again in the contemporary American cinema's celebration of male couples.'[2]

I would like initially to take up this point in relation to the western, whose conventions, it seems to me, function precisely to privilege, examine and celebrate the body of the male.[3] Before doing so, though, it is worth extending Willemen's remarks, making some preliminary points about the functioning of the male and female bodies as inscribed within the apparatus of looking in mainstream cinema in general.

As Willemen points out, the direct object of scopophilic desire need not necessarily be female—it can be and often is, male. Simultaneously, however, it is nevertheless the case that the two objects of the look, male and female, tend to be inscribed and represented differently in this respect. They tend, in particular, to be differentiated according to the degree of eroticism with which they are explicitly marked. What generally happens is that the look at the male is de-eroticised, rendered 'innocent' by inscribing him as the relay point in the looking structure, the point at which the looks are turned towards their ultimate destination, the woman. The erotic component in the look thus tends constantly to be displaced away from the male and on to the female—on to that which is already ideologically defined and accepted as an unproblematic sexual object. In this respect patriarchy does not so much institute the woman as sexual object in the cinema as offer the female body as an accepted and acceptable image on to which to deflect the erotic component in the scopophilic drive.

Turning to the western, and bearing the above remarks in mind, it is worth firstly emphasising the role and function of its basic conventions in opening a space for the inscription of the male as privileged object of the look. These conventions have usually been defined as a function of the genre's setting (best understood perhaps not simply as meaning 'diegetic or referential location' but also as meaning 'the process of solidification': just as the mobile liquid of a jelly sets, so too do the semiotic processes of a narrative text. What they set as is precisely the diegesis or the diegetic image). The setting of the western is the American frontier, which serves both as the mark in relation to which a series of antinomic elements are defined as in opposition and as the axis around which the drama and its conflicts are structured. In his book *Horizons West*, Jim Kitses listed and defined the role of these antinomies as follows:

'Central to the form we have a philosophical dialectic, an ambiguous cluster of meanings and attitudes that pervade the traditional thematic structure of the genre. This shifting ideological play can be described through a series of antinomies, so:

THE WILDERNESS	CIVILISATION
the individual	the community
freedom	restriction
honour	institutions
self-knowledge	illusion
integrity	compromise
self-interest	social responsibility
solipsism	democracy
Nature	Culture
purity	corruption
experience	knowledge
empiricism	legalism
pragmatism	idealism
brutalisation	refinement
savagery	humanity
The West	The East
America	Europe
the frontier	America
equality	class
agrarianism	industrialism
tradition	change
the past	the future'

These in turn find a particular focus in the body of the male hero. They articulate the space of the functioning of what is defined in the genre as the Law, and the space which is defined as outside it, as Other. The body of the hero is situated within a series of other bodies (those of Indians, outlaws, towns-people, farmers and so on) across which this opposition is marked, hence the importance of codes of dress, comportment, movement, adornment, etc. It is marked also across a spatial economy whose polar instances are natural land-

58

scape on the one hand and the township/homestead on the other. Here, again, the body of the hero is located dynamically at the point of their intersection, oscillating between them.

Taking in conjunction the open, exterior space of the former and the more enclosed, internal, linear space of the latter, the western offers maximum scope for variations and permutations on the relations of the male figure to space, light, texture, colour and so on, as well as for variations and permutations on the speed and mode of its movements. It is here, in particular, that the function and the status of the body of the male hero as privileged object of the look can be located. The drama of the western, in its concern to explore various modes of the inscription of Law on the human body, and in its obsession with definitions of masculinity, involves the location of the body of the hero as the object par excellence of its spectacle. Since it is the hero who here engages with the Law, the erotic component of the look at the male is caught in a dialectical movement between the male as ideal father on the one hand and the male as symbolic father on the other, these functions being either mapped on to the hero himself or else distributed variously across a series of male roles. The western can thus be said actually to be 'about' the male half of the Oedipus, in both its symbolic and its erotic dimension, with the Father/Son relationship being articulated across definitions of 'law' and (social) 'order'.

All this is inscribed quite systematically into the westerns of Mann, Peckinpah and Hawks, where the relationship to the problematic of male narcissism and male homosexuality becomes, if not explicit, at least readily apparent. But it is always there in the western in any case, providing one of the bases for its cinematic specificity.

The above remarks are not meant to suggest that in the western there is an exclusive attention to the male. The most important point stemming from Paul Willemen's argument, it seems to me, is that not only is it the case that both sexes can figure as objects of the look, but also that they are each inscribed differently. In any case, however, there is always a balance between the two, one which varies certainly—exactly—in its emphasis (in correlation perhaps with the extent to which any one genre is categorised as 'male' and 'female'), but one which rarely tilts so far in either direction, so to speak, that either male figures or female ones are totally absent. The presence of both the one and the other thus enables the process of the construction of sexual difference to function all the more effectively. Hence if the western, like the war film, predominantly features the male, it also almost always incorporates the direct representation of woman, no matter how 'contrived' or 'clumsy' this may seem in terms of the logic of a given narrative. Similarly, if the melodrama and the musical predominantly tend to feature female characters, they almost always include men too. Indeed, men are crucial to these genres, more so, perhaps, than women are to war films and westerns, which points to the extent to which the representation of women—their definition—always occurs as a function of their relationship to men in these types of narrative regimes.

One of the interesting things about these latter genres is that the stress on women seems simultaneously to involve a 'feminisation' of men. That is to say, given the terms of the inscription of the eroticism of the look outlined above, they involve an eroticisation of the body of the male. They seem to involve, to a certain extent and in certain instances at least, a figuring of the male in terms of codes of cinema, narrative and spectacle more usually reserved for the depiction of women. As Roland Barthes noted:

> 'In every man who speaks of the absence of the other, the feminine declares itself: he who waits and suffers is miraculously feminised—a man is not feminised because he is homosexual, but because he is in love.'[4]

These remarks of Barthes clearly apply to the melodrama, where the agonies of suffering and waiting are experienced predominantly but not exclusively by women, and where, consequently, male lovers can come to acquire attributes of 'the feminine'. Think, for example, of the ways in which Rock Hudson tends to be depicted in Sirk's melodramas (*All That Heaven Allows* and *Magnificent Obsession* in particular) or of the ways in which Charles Farrell is represented in the melodramas of Borzage.

As far as the musical is concerned—although, significantly, in the scenes of singing and dancing which are the moments of spectacle *par excellence*, there is a strong tradition in which it is women alone who are subject to the choreography of the look (the Busby Berkeley films being the obvious example)—it is just as frequently the case that men are thus put on display, participating in these 'celebrations of the body and the voice'.[5]

None of this is to suggest, of course, that difference in these genres is in any way challenged or erased, or that there is some kind of 'subversion' of traditional images of male and female sexual identity. It is merely to suggest some of the more interesting points at which analysis of the production of difference and identity could begin.

The aspects of the two genres I want to mention here are perhaps less directly evident as instances of the inscription/construction of sexual identity and difference. However, in so far as they centre fundamentally on the body, it seems to me that they may be of some significance. In the first of these genres, the horror film, the aspect to which I wish to draw attention concerns the way in which the production of a definition of the monstrous always takes place within the context of the construction of definitions of masculinity and femininity. The interesting point here is that this latter instance of difference (always posed as irreducible, given in the body) must inevitably cross another, that between the monster on the one hand and 'humanity' in general on the other. Since the category of 'the human' is inscribed as a homogeneous one, the construction of categories of sexual difference must inevitably tend to fracture it. The monster, of course, is never totally non-human: it is monstrous precisely because it does possess human traits. It, too, is the site of heterogeneity that threatens the homogeneity of the human. It may therefore, potentially at least, be read as the product of a displacement of the one instance of heterogeneity on to the other.

However, since the monster does possess human traits, it also possesses traits of sexual identity. Its otherness can therefore be conceived in two ways: either as exceeding the categories of masculinity and femininity constructed elsewhere in the films, or else as mixing them dangerously together. In either case, it functions so as to disturb the boundaries of sexual identity and difference. One final point to note, though, is that despite the existence of such disturbances, most monsters tend, in fact, to be defined as 'male', especially in so far as the objects of their desire are almost exclusively women. Simultaneously, it is women who become their primary victims. In this respect, it could well be maintained that it is women's sexuality, that which renders them desirable–but also threatening–to men, which constitutes the real problem that the horror cinema exists to explore, and which constitutes also and ultimately that which is really monstrous.

Lastly, there is one aspect of comedy, in particular of crazy comedy, that I would like briefly to discuss. It concerns gags and the way in which they involve a specific relationship between the body and discourse and therefore language, the symbolic. The term 'gag' originally meant 'interpolation' or 'cascade' and there is clearly a way in which both these meanings retain some degree of value for an understanding of the relationship between the gag and the narrative on the one hand, and of the internal structure of the gags themselves on the other. There is another meaning to the word gag, however, which I want to highlight here: to 'gag' in the sense of blocking the possibilities of vocalisation. The two structural components to this meaning are precisely those of language and body.

As indicated in Chapter Two, comedy is produced in the intersection of a set of distinct discourses or discursive registers, in the clashes and contradictions involved in that intersection and in the dispersions and reconvergences of logic thus engendered. In other words, comedy is produced in the disordering and re-ordering of the relations that constitute the symbolic. A gag is an especially intense instance of these mechanisms and processes and it centres, above all, on the body of the comic, a body which is thus structured exactly as the site of the intersection, as the pivotal component in a process which articulates firstly an interpretation or disturbance in its relations with those discourses it inhabits and encounters and then, secondly, a re-ordering of those relations so that a new equilibrium within and between them is established.

The point to which I want to draw attention is that sexual identity itself is also constructed through modes of the articulation and inscription of the body in the symbolic. The question thus becomes not only one of the extent to which gags (and comedy in general?) focus the components and the mode of construction of sexual identity, but also the extent to which they can be read as instances of the representation of that process itself, together with the disturbances, pressures and repressions it involves. Gags register both the interruption and the reconstitution of subject identity, the interruption and reconstitution of balances of discourse and of balances of subject position within them, locating their point as the human body itself. In the course of the interruptions, as is well known, the body is represented as fragmented/distorted/unco-ordinated/unbalanced; equilibrium is restored as bodily integrity/unity/co-ordination and balance. The issue, then, is that of the degree to which the positions in disruption and in balance are marked as involving gender, the degree to which the identity that is deconstructed and reconstructed can be said to involve sexuality.

61

Notes

[1] For an extended analysis of a number of these aspects, see Stephen Heath's essay 'Difference' in *Screen*, Vol 19, no 2, 1978.

[2] Paul Willemen, 'Voyeurism, The Look and Dwoskin' in *Afterimage*, no 6, 1976, p. 43.

[3] See for instance Paul Willemen's article on the films of Anthony Mann in *Time Out*, no 434, 1978.

[4] Roland Barthes, *Fragments of a Lover's Discourse*, London 1979 (My transl.).

[5] Patricia Mellencamp, 'Spectacle and Spectator: Looking Through the American Musical Comedy' in *Cinetracts*, Vol 1, no 2, 1977.

Appendix B: Teaching Genre

Much of the original impetus for the body of work on genre discussed in the opening chapter of this book derived from an educational context. In seeking to construct film as a coherent discipline that could be introduced into schools, colleges and universities, considerable effort went into the analysis, discussion and specification of notions like authorship and genre in particular. It is from the basis provided by this body of work, developed initially in the late sixties and early seventies, that, by and large, courses on genre are taught today.

In so far as I have sought to challenge and to extend that basis, the formulations proposed in this book clearly do have some implications for the ways in which genre is taught, as indeed for the ways in which mainstream narrative cinema is approached and conceptualised. In this appendix, I want to indicate, briefly, what some of these implications might be and to offer suggestions for the way in which one might engage in classrooms, as well as in exhibition situations or seminars, with those implications.

Throughout, the aim of this monograph has been to provide not simply an understanding of genre, but rather, and simultaneously, it has been to provide an understanding of genre as an intrinsic part of the cinematic institution and an understanding of the cinematic institution through an examination of genre. Any course on genre must, in my view, adopt a similar aim. That is to say, genre study is not there to be taught for its own sake, so to speak, nor is it there simply to enrich the pleasures and meanings to be derived from individual genre films. Rather, it is there to provide knowledge about cinema and the way it functions as a social institution.

The approach I have taken has been to focus on the fact that genres produce a regulated variety of cinema, a contained and controlled heterogeneity that explores and exploits the optimum potentiality of cinema's resources and, in particular, the narrative system it has adopted as its aesthetic and ideological basis. From here, I have attempted to indicate firstly some of the discursive characteristics of the various genres as they relate to and derive from the characteristics of mainstream narrative film and, secondly, some of the mechanics involved in the constitution and perpetuation of genres as distinct discursive entities. If something like this perspective is to be inscribed into the structure of a study programme on genre, it seems to me crucial that there should be some space devoted to an examination of the mainstream narrative system *per se* and that a variety of genres be discussed. Regarding the latter point, whatever the merits might be of taking a specific genre and examining that genre in depth, it is absolutely crucial that the function of genre be addressed and that therefore the fact and the nature of the variety of genres be brought to the fore. The best way of doing this, in my view, is to present and discuss that variety. From here, and only from here, can a proper analysis of any one genre ensue. Even here, though, one should be careful not to privilege the genre selected. Too often, it seems to me, the western and the gangster film have taken precedence over the other genres. Some of the theoretical reasons for this have been discussed in the first chapter of the book. Existing approaches may well provide valuable insights concerning some of the elements of those specific genres, but they also tend both to undervalue other genres (especially the horror film, the musical and the epic) and, perhaps more importantly, to lose sight of the role of genre in general within the functioning of the cinematic institution as a whole.

The following is an attempt to indicate, first, what the basis for a structure of a genre study programme might be and, secondly, what kinds of extracts and written material might be of use. The problem with providing models of this kind is that they tend to be regarded as prescriptive whereas they are intended as suggestions to be adapted and modified according to the specific teaching or programming situations involved. In order to minimise this problem, these suggestions are outlined in skeletal forms and the examples of titles or extracts are, I hope, sufficiently extensive to allow for the required flexibility.

I. As indicated above, the first part of the course should attempt to engage with some of the general characteristics of the mainstream narrative film. Within this, I include such elements as the structure of narrative, with its initial stasis, its processes of interruption and inauguration of drama and its moment of resolution, the re-inscription of stasis and equilibrium. From here something can be indicated about the ways in which the processes of the drama itself are contained by repetitions, rhymes and echoes at the levels of both 'form' and 'content'. Finally, but importantly, some of the conventions involved in the cinematic articulation of narrative should be discussed. Such conventions include rules of editing and continuity, the construction of a homogeneous fictional time and space, and the subordination of the effects and potentialities of cinema as a medium for narration and the articulation of a single diegesis. As with the rest of the course, the extent to which one will be able to examine these questions will depend upon factors of time and of the age group with which one is dealing. Nevertheless, it is important that they be broached as a basis for discussion of the variations that genres work upon the conventions indicated. The best way, in my view, of highlighting the fact that these conventions are conventions is through comparison and contrast. So one would proceed by discussing an instance or several instances of classical narration and then proceed from there to introduce counter instances.

Since teaching, in my view, should in general proceed from identification to separation and analysis, the instance of mainstream narrative chosen as a starter to the course should be one with which students will identify, one which will 'hold' and interest them. Obviously, the exact choice of film should be determined according to the nature of the teaching situation, but it is worth mentioning the following films since they have been analysed at some length and since the nature of the analyses can easily be integrated into the kind of approach I have taken in the book. Full bibliographic details for the written material mentioned can be found in the bibliography closing this monograph.

Citizen Kane: extensively analysed in *Film Reader* no 1, now out of print but still available for consultation in the BFI library.

The Big Sleep: discussed specifically from a teaching point of view by Gill Davies in her article *Teaching about Narrative.*

Touch of Evil: discussed in great detail by Stephen Heath in a two part article *Film and System: Terms of Analysis.*

Pursued: analysed by Paul Willemen in the Edinburgh/BFI book on Raoul Walsh edited by Phil Hardy.

It is also worth mentioning Stephen Heath's remarks on *Jaws* in *Framework* no 4 and the remarks on *The Maltese Falcon* contained in Bordwell and Thompson's essay on *Space and Narrative in the Films of Ozu,* where they discuss the film as an example of classic narrative (pp. 42–3). Finally, with regard to the workings of specific individual scenes as instances of mainstream narrative, Raymond Bellour's article *The Obvious and the Code* analysing a sequence from *The Big Sleep* and Nick Browne's essay on *Stagecoach* are both detailed and useful.

In teaching about narrative, extracts from the opening and/or ending of films can be particularly useful. The following list is from those currently available from the BFI Educational Advisory Service (EAS):

Openings: *All That Heaven Allows; Broken Arrow; Dirty Harry; Farewell My Lovely; I Am a Fugitive From a Chain Gang; Kiss Me Deadly; Letter From an Unknown Woman; Madigan; Marnie; Once Upon a Time in the West; The Godfather; The Killers ('46 and '64); The Public Enemy; The Lusty Men; To Have and Have Not; Winchester '73.*

Endings: *Anatomy of a Murder; Brute Force; Double Indemnity; I Am a Fugitive From a Chain Gang; Mr. Deeds Goes to Town; Once Upon a Time in the West; River of No Return; Stella Dallas; Targets; The Best Years of Our Lives; The Birds; The Far Country; The Line Up; To Have and Have Not; Touch of Evil.*

As regards examples of strategies that depart from the conventions of mainstream narrative, the following extracts and features might be useful:

Extracts: *Breathless; Bande à Part; British Sounds; Early Spring; Hiroshima Mon Amour; Man With a Movie Camera; Masculin-Féminin; October: Pierrot le Fou; Tokyo Story; Two or Three Things I Know About Her; Une Femme Mariée; Weekend.*

Shorts and features: *After Lumière; Machorka Muff; The Bridegroom, the Comedienne and the Pimp; Un Chien Andalou; L'Age d'Or; Wavelength; Zorns Lemma; Vent d'Est.*

Obviously, the choice of material used here very much depends on the specific context. Equally obviously, the bulk of avant garde films could have been included together with the collected works of Godard. The above examples have been selected because all, in one way or another and to a greater or lesser extent, present traces of conventional plot and narrative, thus providing suitable examples on the basis of which differential comparisons can be made and discussed. The one exception is *Zorns Lemma*, where an alternative means of sequencing images is clearly and accessibly inscribed into the film. Regarding one or two of the titles included here, it is worth mentioning the following written material which in each case discusses the ways these films differ from mainstream narrative: for the Godard films: Steve Crofts' BFI Study Unit on Godard; E. Branigan essay on *Two or Three Things I Know About Her*; Julia Lesage's *Visual Distancing in Godard*; Colin McCabe's *The Politics of Separation*; M. C. Ropars' *Form and Substance or the Avatars of Narrative*; Peter Wollen's *Counter Cinema: Vent d'Est*. For the two films by Ozu, see Bordwell and Thompson's *Space and Narrative in the Films of Ozu*. See also Crofts and Rose's article on *Man With A Movie Camera*, M. C. Ropars' essay on *October*, Phillip Drummond on *Un Chien Andalou* and Mick Eaton's *The Avant Garde and Narrative* where he discusses *Zorns Lemma*. A concise and useful survey of the strategies of the various avant gardes *vis-à-vis* mainstream cinema is contained in Phillip Drummond's essay *Notions of Avant Garde Cinema* in the *Film as Film* catalogue published by the Arts Council of Great Britain. Together with Stephen Heath's *Repetition Time: Notes around 'Structural Materialist Films'*, Drummond's article could provide the basis for an approach to much avant garde work in so far as it contrasts with strategies of mainstream narrative cinema.

II. Having drawn out a number of the basic characteristics of mainstream narrative, genre, or rather a range of genres, can be introduced. The precise order and extent to which this is done will, again, depend on circumstances. Two points need to be strongly brought out. The first is that genres are varieties of mainstream cinema, the second is that they are processes articulated within a precise economy of repetition and difference. There needs to be, therefore, a sufficient number of genres included for the first point to be made and enough material within any one genre for the second. Extracts are obviously extremely useful here. In the list of titles below I have grouped those extracts available under generic headings and indicated where they are included within BFI Study Units on the genre concerned. I have specified books and articles where they share something of the approach adopted in this monograph or where they can be integrated into it. Unfortunately, a number of these are in French, though wherever possible I have referred to translations. Finally, I have listed feature films currently available on 16 mm either where the film in question has been referred to in detail or on a number of occasions in this monograph or where there is little or no extract material available:

Comedy

Extracts: *Battle of the Century; Born Yesterday; Bringing Up Baby; Dr. Strangelove; Easy Street; The Lavender Hill Mob; Man in the White Suit; Mr. Deeds Goes to Town; Oh For a Man; Sullivan's Travels; The Vagabond; What's New Pussycat?*

Features:	*Cocoanuts; Duck Soup; A Night at the Opera; The Disorderly Orderly; To Be Or Not To Be; Trouble in Paradise; The General.*
Books:	J. P. Coursodon, *Keaton et Cie*; J. P. Lebel, *Buster Keaton*; F. Mars, *Le Gag*; C. Johnston and P. Willemen, *Frank Tashlin.*
Articles:	J. Ellis, *Made in Ealing*; A. Garel, *Le Burlesque*; P. Willemen, *The Lubitsch Touch* (a complete version of this somewhat mangled article in *Time Out* is available from the BFI/EAS).

Detective film

Extracts:	*Coogan's Bluff; Dirty Harry; Madigan; Crossfire; Farewell My Lovely; Kiss Me Deadly; Klute; Laura; On Dangerous Ground; Out of the Past; The Big Heat; The Maltese Falcon.*
Features:	*Chinatown; The Big Sleep.*
Articles:	Todorov's essays *The Typology of Detective Fiction* and *Introduction to Verisimilitude* in *The Poetics of Prose*; Marc Vernet's contribution to *Lectures du Film*; Mike Westlake's *The Classic Detective Genre* to be published shortly in *Framework*.

Epic

Extract:	*Spartacus.*
Features:	this list is fairly long because there is only one extract available and little serious work has been done on this genre. It should be borne in mind that most of these films are very long and may pose considerable timetabling problems. *Barabbas* ('62); *Ben Hur* ('60); *Cleopatra* ('34 and '63); *Helen of Troy; Hercules; King of Kings* ('21 and '61); *Quo Vadis* ('51); *The Bible; The Giant of Marathon; The Robe* (available only in standard format although it was the first CinemaScope film); *The Ten Commandments* ('56).

Phantasy/Adventure

As with the epic, there is little extract material available.

Features:	*Aladdin's Lamp; Atlantis the Lost Continent; Captain Sinbad; Jason and the Argonauts; Son of Sinbad; Sinbad and the Eye of the Tiger; The Adventures of Sinbad; The Thief of Bagdad* ('40).
Books:	René Predal's *Le Cinéma Fantastique* and Gérard Lenne's *Le Cinéma Fantastique et ses Mythologies* are useful. Todorov's book on the literary phantastic is the most productive work in existence about this genre.

Gangster film

The BFI Teacher's Study Guide no 2, edited by Tom Ryall, contains the following extracts: *Dirty Harry; High Sierra; Murder Inc.; On the Waterfront; Portrait of a Mobster; The Godfather; The House on 92nd Street; The Public Enemy; The Rise and Fall of Legs Diamond; The Roaring Twenties; Le Samourai; The St. Valentine's Day Massacre; Scarface; Underworld USA.*

Other extracts available: *Baby Face Nelson; Gambling House; G-Men; Little Caesar; Machine Gun Kelly; Racket Busters; The Harder They Fall; The Line Up.*

Article: Todorov's essay on the detective genre in *The Poetics of Prose.*

Book: Colin McArthur's *Underworld USA.*

Horror

There will soon be a BFI Resource Pack, available from the BFI/EAS, edited by Dave Pirie. It will contain the following extracts from Hammer films:

Dracula; Dracula Prince of Darkness; Brides of Dracula; The Satanic Rites of Dracula; Taste the Blood of Dracula; Plague of the Zombies; The Devil Rides Out; Hound of the Baskervilles; The Mummy.

Other extracts available: *Cat People; Dracula* ('30); *Frankenstein* ('31); *Legend of the Werewolf; Peeping Tom; Psycho; Rosemary's Baby; The Tomb of Ligeia.*

Books: Lenne's *Le Cinéma Fantastique et ses Mythologies*; Predal's *Le Cinéma Fantastique*; Todorov's *The Fantastic*; Bessière's *Le Récit Fantastique.*

Articles: J. F. Tarnowski's contributions to *Positif* and Roger Dadoun's essay in *Enclitic.*

Melodrama

Extracts: *All That Heaven Allows; Foolish Wives; Hearts of the World; Letter From an Unknown Woman; Mildred Pierce; A Streetcar Named Desire; Stella Dallas; The Little Foxes; The Magnificent Ambersons; Written on the Wind.*

Features: *Rebel Without a Cause; Three Comrades; Home From the Hill; The Cobweb; The Bad and the Beautiful; Two Weeks in Another Town.*

Articles: T. Elsaesser's *Tales of Sound and Fury*; G. Pollock, G. Nowell-Smith and S. Heath's dossier on melodrama in *Screen*; Laura Mulvey's *Notes on Sirk and Melodrama.*

Book: Mulvey and Halliday's book on Douglas Sirk.

Musical

A BFI Study Unit, edited by Richard Dyer, contains the following extracts: *Gold Diggers of 1933; Funny Face; Sweet Charity; The Gay Divorcee.*

Other extracts available: *Carmen Jones; Darling Lili; On A Clear Day You Can See Forever; Top Hat.*

Features: *Brigadoon; Meet Me in St. Louis; The Bandwagon; The Pirate; On the Town; Singin' in the Rain.*

Articles: T. Elsaesser's *The Musical and Vincente Minnelli* in *The Brighton Film Review*; Michel Marie's essay on musical comedy in Vernet's *Lectures du Film*; P. Mellencamp's essay in *Cinetracts.*

Science Fiction
The Resource Pack edited by Dave Pirie, shortly to be available from the BFI and mentioned in connection with the horror genre, also contains the following science fiction extracts: *Quatermass 2; The Damned; The Quatermass Experiment; X The Unknown.*
Other extracts available: *The Day the Earth Caught Fire; The Lost World.*
Features: *Creature from the Black Lagoon; It Came From Outer Space; Invasion of the Body Snatchers* ('56); *The Incredible Shrinking Man; The Thing From Another World; Them.*
Books and articles: the same material mentioned in relation to the horror genre is relevant to discussion of science fiction.

Thriller
Extracts: *Beyond a Reasonable Doubt; Double Indemnity; Frenzy; Shadow of a Doubt; The Killers* ('46 and '64); *They Live By Night.*
Features: *Beyond a Reasonable Doubt; North by Northwest.*
Articles: see Todorov's contribution to the study of the detective genre and the problem of verisimilitude in *The Poetics of Prose.*

Western
The BFI Study Unit on the western, edited by Ed Buscombe, contains the feature *The Far Country* and the following extracts: *Man Without a Star; Union Pacific; Winchester '73.*
Other extracts available: *Cowboy; Broken Arrow; Major Dundee; My Darling Clementine; Once Upon a Time in the West; Rancho Notorious; River of No Return; She Wore a Yellow Ribbon; Stagecoach; The Big Sky; The Covered Wagon; The Far Country; The Gunfighter; The James Brothers; The Man From Laramie; The Wonderful Country; Two Rode Together; Wagonmaster; Where The River Bends.*
Books: Cawelti's *The Six Gun Mystique*; Kitses' *Horizons West*; Leutrat's *Le Western.*
Articles: P. Willemen's *Modern Mann.*

III. *Reminders*
It is important that issues to do with the relation between genre and industry be ✓ posed throughout any study programme and that the point be made from the outset that narrative is mainstream cinema's primary commodity. At the conclusion of a programme, it is important to draw these issues together in a more systematic way and to link them to points about cinema as institution, so that genre is firmly placed within a regime of discursive and economic relations. There is a huge amount of very diverse material on the industry, but not so much about the nature of its commodities in their function as instances of discourse. John Ellis' article *The Institution of Cinema* is a useful starting point. ✓ Metz's *The Imaginary Signifier* is, of course, crucial for raising questions about cinema as a specific discursive institution and should inform the course or

programme as a whole. Finally, as regards genre and the industry particularly at the moment of production, the material available from the BFI on *Legend of the Werewolf*, including the book about the making of the film, is of some value. In so far as the overall economics of mainstream cinema are concerned, though, some understanding of the functioning of a capitalist economy will have to be provided. Here one is likely to have to turn to material that is by and large outside the field of 'film studies'.

Bibliography

Karl Abraham	— *Selected Papers,* London 1978.
Roland Barthes	— *Image, Music, Text,* edited by Stephen Heath, London 1978.
	— *S/Z,* London 1975.
	— *The Pleasure of the Text,* London 1976.
	— *Fragments of a Lover's Discourse,* London 1979.
Raymond Bellour	— 'The Obvious and the Code' in *Screen,* Vol 15, no 2.
Alain Bergala	— 'Dora and The Magic Lantern' in *Cahiers du Cinéma,* no 287.
Irène Bessière	— *Le Récit Fantastique,* Paris 1970.
David Bordwell and Kristin Thompson	— 'Space and Narrative in the films of Ozu' in *Screen,* Vol 17, no 2.
Edward Branigan	— 'The Articulation of Colour in a Filmic System: Two or Three Things I Know About Her' in *Wide Angle,* Vol 1, no 3.
Nick Browne	— 'The Spectator in the Text: The Rhetoric of Stagecoach' in *Film Quarterly,* Vol 22, no 3.
Ed Buscombe	— 'The Idea of Genre in the American Cinema' in *Screen,* Vol 11, no 2.
	— *BFI Study Unit no 12: The Western,* London 1971.
	— *Making Legend of the Werewolf,* London 1976.
John Cawelti	— *The Six Gun Mystique,* Bowling Green, Ohio, no date.
Jean-Pierre Coursodon	— *Keaton et Cie,* Paris 1961.
Steve Crofts	— *BFI Study Unit no 15: Godard,* London 1972.
S. Crofts and Olivia Rose	— 'An Essay Towards Man With A Movie Camera' in *Screen,* Vol 18, no 1.
Roger Dadoun	— 'Fetishism in the Horror Film' in *Enclitic,* Vol 1, no 2.
Gill Davies	— 'Teaching about Narrative' in *Screen Education,* no 29.
Phillip Drummond	— 'Textual Space in Un Chien Andalou' in *Screen,* Vol 18, no 3.
	— 'Notions of Avant Garde Cinema' in *Film as Film —* Catalogue, London 1979.
Danièle Dubroux	— 'Fedora' in *Cahiers du Cinéma,* no 294 (extracts available in English translation from BFI EAS).
Richard Dyer	— *BFI Study Unit no 16: The Musical,* London 1975.
Antony Easthope	— 'Notes on Genre' in *Screen Education,* no 32/33.

Mick Eaton	– 'The Avant Garde and Narrative' in *Screen*, Vol 19, no 2.
John Ellis	✓ – 'The Institution of Cinema' in *Edinburgh '77 Magazine*, edited by Claire Johnston.
	– 'Made in Ealing' in *Screen*, Vol 16, no 1.
	– 'Writing, Filming and Context: A Reply to Mark Nash' in *Screen Education*, no 27.
Thomas Elsaesser	– 'The Musical' in *Brighton Film Review*, no 18.
	– 'Tales of Sound and Fury' in *Monogram*, no 4.
	– 'Vincente Minnelli' in *Brighton Film Review*, no 15.
✓ Film Reader no 1	✓ – 'Semiotics and Citizen Kane' by Peter Wollen, Steve Fagin, Joe Hill, William Crouch, Garner Simmons, Patricia Erens, Jay Bartush (see also BFI Study Unit no 9: Orson Welles).
	– 'The Western' by Garner Simmons.
Alain Garel	– 'Le Burlesque' in *Image et Son*, nos 324 and 326.
✓ Stephen Heath	– 'Notes on Suture' in *Screen*, Vol 18, no 4.
	– 'Film and System: Terms of Analysis' in *Screen*, Vol 16, nos 1 and 2.
	– 'Film Performance' in *Cinetracts*, Vol 1, no 2.
	✓ – 'Repetition Time: Notes Around "Structural Materialist Films"' in *Wide Angle*, Vol 2, no 3.
	– 'Narrative Space' in *Screen*, Vol 17, no 4.
	✓ – 'Dossier on Melodrama' in *Screen*, Vol 18, no 2.
	– 'Anata Mo' in *Screen*, Vol 17, no 4.
	– 'The Question Oshima' in *Wide Angle*, Vol 2, no 1.
	– 'Difference' in *Screen*, Vol 19, no 2.
	– 'Jaws' in *Framework*, no 4.
	– (Ed.) *Image, Music, Text* by Roland Barthes, London 1978.
Jim Kitses	– *Horizons West*, London 1969.
Jacques Lacan	– *The Four Fundamental Principles of Psychoanalysis*, Harmondsworth 1979.
Jean-Pierre Lebel	– *Buster Keaton,* London 1967.
Gerard Lenne	– *Le Cinéma Fantastique et ses Mythologies*, Paris 1970.
Julia Lesage	– 'Visual Distancing in Godard' in *Wide Angle*, Vol 1, no 3.
Jean-Louis Leutrat	– *Le Western*, Paris 1973.
Yuri Lotman	– *La Structure du Texte Artistique*, Paris 1973.
Colin McArthur	– *Underworld USA*, London 1972.
	– *Iconography and Iconology*, Seminar Paper BFI/SEFT, 1973.
Colin McCabe	– 'The Politics of Separation' in *Screen*, Vol 16, no 4.
Octave Mannoni	– *Clefs pour l'Imaginaire*, Paris 1969.

François Mars	– *Le Gag*, Paris 1964.
Patricia Mellencamp	– 'Spectacle and Spectator – Looking Through the American Musical Comedy' in *Cinetracts*, Vol 1, no 2.
Christian Metz	– 'The Imaginary Signifier' in *Screen*, Vol 16, no. 2.
	– 'Histoire/Discourse – A Note Towards Two Voyeurisms' in *Edinburgh '76 Magazine*, edited by P. Hardy, C. Johnston and P. Willemen.
	– 'Image et Cinéma' in *Essais sur la Signification au Cinéma*, Vol 3, Paris 1975.
	– 'Trucage et Cinéma' in *Essais sur la Signification au Cinéma*, Vol 2, Paris 1972 (Inadequate English version in *Critical Enquiry*, Vol 2, no 4).
J. A. Miller	– 'Suture (Elements of the Logic of the Signifier)' in *Screen*, Vol 16, no 3.
Laura Mulvey	– 'Visual Pleasure and Narrative Cinema' in *Screen*, Vol 16, no 3.
	– *Douglas Sirk*, edited by L. Mulvey and J. Halliday, Edinburgh 1974.
	– 'You don't know what is happening do you, Mr. Jones' in *Spare Rib*, no 8.
	– 'Notes on Sirk and Melodrama' in *Movie*, no 25.
Geoffrey Nowell-Smith ✓	– 'Dossier on Melodrama' in *Screen*, Vol 18, no 2.
Jean Pierre Oudart	– 'Cinema and Suture' in *Screen*, Vol 18, no 4.
Victor Perkins	– *Film As Film*, Harmondsworth 1972.
Griselda Pollock	– 'Dossier on Melodrama' in *Screen*, Vol 18, no 2.
René Predal	– *Le Cinéma Fantastique*, Paris 1970.
Douglas Pye	✓ – 'Genre and Movies' in *Movie*, no 20.
M. C. Ropars	✓ – 'Form and Substance or the Avatars of Narrative' in *Focus on Godard*, edited by R. S. Brown, New Jersey, 1972.
	– 'The Overture of October' in *Enclitic*, Vol 2, no 2 and Vol 3, no 1.
Tom Ryall	✓ – 'The Notion of Genre' in *Screen*, Vol 11, no 2.
	– 'Teaching Through Genre' in *Screen Education*, no 17.
	– *BFI Teacher's Study Guide no 2: Gangster Film*, London 1978.
Jean-François Tarnowski	– 'Les Voies du Silence' in *Positif*, no 177.
	– 'Approche et Definition(s) du Fantastique et de la Science Fiction Cinématographique' in *Positif*, nos 195–6 and 208–9.
Tzvetan Todorov	– *The Poetics of Prose*, Cornell University Press, 1977.
	– *The Fantastic*, Cleveland, Ohio, 1975.
Marc Vernet (ed)	– *Lectures du Film*, Paris 1975.

Mike Westlake	— 'Dating the Movies' in *North By Northwest*, no 8.
	— 'The Classic Detective Genre: TV Detectives of the Seventies' (to be published in *Framework*).
	— 'Genre and Subject' (unpublished Seminar Paper, 1979).
Sheila Whitaker	— 'To Be Or Not To Be' in *Framework*, no 5.
Paul Willemen	— 'Notes on Subjectivity' in *Screen*, Vol 19, no 1.
	— 'Voyeurism, The Look and Dwoskin' in *Afterimage*, no 6.
	— 'Notes Towards the Construction of Readings of Tourneur' in *Jacques Tourneur*, edited by P. Willemen and C. Johnston, Edinburgh 1975.
	— 'Tashlin's Method: An Hypothesis' in *Frank Tashlin*, edited by P. Willemen and C. Johnston, Edinburgh 1973.
	— 'Pursued: The Fugitive Subject' in *Raoul Walsh*, edited by Phil Hardy, Edinburgh 1974.
	— 'Modern Mann' in *Time Out*, no 434.
	— 'The Lubitsch Touch' in *Time Out*, no 455 (complete text of this article is available from BFI/EAS).
Peter Wollen	— 'Counter Cinema: Vent d'Est' in *Afterimage*, no 4.
	— *BFI Study Unit: Orson Welles*, London 1969.